PANDORA'S BOX

CORPORATE POWER, FREE TRADE AND CANADIAN EDUCATION

BY

JOHN CALVERT

WITH

LARRY KUEHN

370
.19
0971
C167

Canadian Cataloguing in Publication Data

Calvert, John, 1947–
Pandora's box

(Our schools/our selves monograph series ; no. 13)
Includes bibliographical references.
ISBN 0–921908–14–8

1. Education – Canada. 2. Education – Economic aspects – Canada.
3. Free trade – Canada. 4. Free trade – North America.
5. Canada – Commercial treaties. I. Our Schools/Our Selves Education
Foundation. II. Title. IV. Series.

LA412.7.C35 1993   370'.971   C93–095082–8

This book is published by Our Schools/Our Selves Education Foundation, 1698 Gerrard Street East, Toronto, Ontario, M4L 2B2.

For subscribers to *Our Schools/Our Selves: a magazine for Canadian education activists*, this is issue #30, the sixth issue of volume 4.

The subscription series Our Schools/Our Selves (ISSN 0840-7339) is published 6 times a year. Publication Mail Registration Number 8010. Mailed at Centre Ville, Montréal, Québec.

Design and typesetting: Tobin M^ac^Intosh.

Cover drawing: Vidal Alcolea.

Our Schools/Our Selves production: Nick Marchese (Co-ordinating Editor), Loren Lind, Doug Little, Bob Luker, Tobin MacIntosh, George Martell (Executive Editor), Susan Prentice, Satu Repo, Harry Smaller.

Printed in Canada by La maîtresse d'école inc., Montréal, Québec.
Copyright © John Calvert
July/August 1993

Acknowledgements

The authors would like to express their appreciation to a number of people who have made this book possible. First, and foremost, we would like to thank George Martell, who pushed, cajoled and guilted us into making the commitment last spring to expand our brief article on the impact of NAFTA on education into this larger book. George's enthusiasm is infectious and his support has been of enormous benefit. Nick Marchese, our co-ordinating editor, patiently accepted all our excuses for the delays and missed deadlines for the manuscript. Our editor, Loren Lind, did a marvellous job of plugging the gaps and holes in our arguments and tossing out material of questionable value.

We must say a special thanks to the organizers of the conference on NAFTA and higher education held last February at the Labor Education and Research Center, Evergreen State College in Olympia, Washington. In particular we would like to mention Dan Leahy and Helen Lee. Not only was this conference a great inspiration to us: the voluminous conference kit was an invaluable resource. We mined it ruthlessly — hopefully to good effect.

We would also like to thank a number of people whose advice, suggestions and support have greatly assisted us in this project. David Clanfield helped edit several chapters and provided useful comments. Jim Turk provided us with a large amount of material, much of which ended up incorporated into the manuscript. Noel McGinn made some important suggestions on our Mexican chapter as did Maria Theresa Gutierrez and Jack Warnock. Roseanne Moran compiled much useful information on the privatization of training at the community college level. Marcie Cohen helped us understand the policy orientation of the federal government in setting up the Canada Labour Force Development Board.

David Langille gave us some very helpful ideas about researching the role of the Business Council on National Issues and the Corporate-Higher Education Forum. Catherine Remus shared with us a draft of a paper she was writing on NAFTA and post-secondary education. Bruce Campbell took the time to read much of the manuscript and gave us a number of useful suggestions regarding the appropriate interpretation of the text of NAFTA. David Noble reviewed the chapter on post-secondary education and we have incorporated a number of his suggestions in the final text. Janice Newson's work and comments were of great assistance. Colleen Fuller read substantial parts of the manuscript and contributed a number of suggestions concerning the parallels between education and health care. David Robbins, of OPIRG, sent us some excellent material on business-university connections. Kelly Lamrock kindly read the chapter on post-secondary education.

Many others have made suggestions in developing this work. These include: Ray Worley, Elsie McMurtry, Jim MacFarlan and other staff at the British Columbia Teachers' Federation; Blair Redlin, Morna Ballantyne, Stan Marshall and Richard Balnis at the Canadian Union of Public Employees; and Marjorie Cohen and other members of the Department of Political Science at Simon Fraser University.

Of course, the views and statements in the book are the sole responsibility of the authors.

Contents

Preface		*1*
Chapter 1	Opening Pandora's Box	*5*
Chapter 2	NAFTA: What's In The Deal?	*12*
Chapter 3	Free Trade And The U.S. Model Of Education	*49*
Chapter 4	NAFTA And Education In Mexico	*65*
Chapter 5	The 'Americanization' Of Canadian Education	*89*
Chapter 6	NAFTA And Post-Secondary Education In Canada	*104*
Chapter 7	Privatization Of Training: The Tory Attack On Public Training Programs	*136*
Chapter 8	NAFTA And The Public Sector/Conclusion	*150*
Notes		*161*

Preface

This book is about free trade and its impact on education in Canada. It is also about the rapidly growing influence of business interests in restructuring our educational system. Its purpose is to analyze the powerful economic, political and social forces which have been set in motion, or are being reinforced, by free trade. It documents the profound educational changes now taking place as a result of the Canada-U.S. Free Trade Agreement (FTA) — changes which are already resulting in the rapid commercialization and privatization of our educational system. And it attempts to predict the impact of the proposed North American Free Trade Agreement (NAFTA) on the future of education in Canada.

Although our book assesses the specific educational impacts of free trade, these occur within a broader political, economic and social context. In our introductory chapter, we provide a brief account of the process by which NAFTA was passed by the federal government. This shows the intentions of its authors and the direction they wish to see Canadian society — and Canadian education — take in the coming years. There was virtually no consultation with the educational community or the wider public by the federal government during the period it was completing NAFTA. Subsequent concerns raised by teachers' organizations and others were brushed aside as irrelevant or unimportant. The federal government attempted to persuade Canadians that the deal would have virtually no impact on educational or other public services, despite the many references to such services in the text.

Yet a growing body of evidence shows that free trade directly affects education. To understand these effects, we have to examine the parts of the chapters of the FTA and NAFTA that sweep in education as part of their broader treatment of services, investment, telecommunications, intellectual property and the public sector. Chapter Two focuses on the specifics of the trade deals and their impact on educational services. It documents the practical impact of some of the key provisions of the FTA on our educational services thus far. Further, it assesses the likely impact of the many new — and much stronger — provisions included in NAFTA.

NAFTA is intended to integrate Canada into a new set of economic relations in the hemisphere. The integration and harmonization of our economy and our public sector gives rise to the question: Integration into what? So, we need to look at the educational systems which will serve as models for this integration. This means, principally, that of the United States. The U.S. educational system differs significantly from ours. A close examination of that system and its recent history suggests that we are now in the process of copying many of its trends, with consequences which many Canadians will find disturbing.

Our third chapter presents an overview of the U.S. primary and secondary educational system. American education is more commercial than ours. Private education plays a much greater role. It is much more segregated by racial and class lines. It is also characterized by massive inequalities. Our account of the U.S. system presents a picture of decaying, cash-starved public schools co-existing with a growing — and racially segregated — elite private system for the rich and the middle classes who have fled to the suburbs from the inner cities.

In addition, U.S. public educational programs have been shaped to accommodate the needs of business to a degree not (yet) present in Canada. The dominance of competitive business values has enabled a predatory private sector to tap into the major sources of public education finance. Across the U.S., profit-making schools have sprung up over the past two decades. These focus on the job-specific needs of U.S. industry to the exclusion of broader educational goals and values.

Insofar as free trade will push Canada towards privatizing and commercializing education, it represents a significant change from Canada's traditions.

The influence of U.S. educational practices is not restricted to Canada. Mexico, currently the third partner in NAFTA, is undergoing wrenching social and economic changes as the government of President Carlos Salinas de Gortari attempts to prepare the country for hemispheric free trade. The restructuring of Mexican education has been a top priority for the current Mexican government. Our fourth chapter looks at recent and proposed changes to Mexican education.

Many of these changes now occurring in Mexico bear remarkable — indeed uncanny — parallels to Canada's recent experience under the FTA. The commercialization and privatization of education is being pushed ahead at an accelerating pace. At the same time, the federal government's role in funding is being cut back. Education finance is being downloaded on fiscally-strapped state governments in a manner resembling the Canadian federal government's cuts to provincial transger payments for health, education and social assistance. Mexico provides a perspective through which we can evaluate the longer-term impact of hemispheric integration on education.

The Canadian system of education is not one system but a mosaic of programs. Although our constitution places education largely within the provincial domain, federal, provincial and local governments are all deeply involved. And, there are a number of public institutions such as universities which, although publicly funded, have a large degree of independence from government. Free trade will affect the various parts of our system in different ways. The impact on daycare will differ, to some degree, from the effect on primary and secondary education. Similarly, the impact on adult training and skills development will be somewhat different from the effect on universities and colleges.

Consequently, we have devoted the next three chapters to examining the ways in which three central components of our educational system will be affected by free trade. Chapter Five examines primary and secondary education. Chapter Six reviews the impact on post-secondary educational institutions.

And, Chapter Seven discusses the implications for training programs.

Education is part of Canada's public sector, and Canada's educational system is overwhelmingly a public system. Consequently, changes to the mandate, financing, management and general operation of Canada's public sector will impact on educational services. Chapter Eight presents a broader analysis of the effect of free trade on our public institutions. The FTA and, even more, NAFTA impose a variety of conditions on how our public programs and services will be carried out in the future. These restrictions constitute a significant break with Canada's 'public' culture and point to the likely abandonment of much of our historic approach to public services and programs.

Our basic objective in writing this book is to encourage the educational community to make this issue a focus for a major public debate in the coming months and years. At the time of writing we do not know whether NAFTA will succeed or fail in the U.S. Congress. Nor can we predict the outcome of the Canadian federal election to be held in the autumn of 1993. We believe that in both cases there will be opportunities for those opposed to free trade to make their voices heard.

Our book does not purport to be the last word on free trade and education. We have been constrained both by our own limited resources and by our belief that there should be a serious discussion of the educational impact of free trade before Canada is permanently locked into this course of action. This latter concern has pushed us into completing this manuscript perhaps more quickly than we would, ideally, have liked. Yet we hope what we have written will encourage those concerned about Canada's educational system to think seriously about the negative impact NAFTA is likely to have on the future of education in this country.

Although we have a point of view — we are critical of the deal — we recognize that we do not have the full answers for many of the significant questions provoked by free trade. If, however, we succeed in encouraging a widespread debate, our purpose in writing this book will have been fulfilled.

Chapter One

Opening Pandora's Box

The North American Free Trade Agreement (NAFTA) is a massive document which maps out the direction of social, economic and public policy in Canada for future generations.[1] Misleadingly named a 'trade deal', it is more accurately described as a 'new economic constitution' for the Americas — a constitution with implications more far-reaching than any Charlottetown Accord.

NAFTA, like the Canada-U.S. Free Trade Agreement (FTA) before it, treats many of our social institutions, including education, as service commodities that must be opened up to the competitive pressures of the marketplace.[2] The assumption that educational services can — indeed should — be treated as economic commodities constitutes a fundamental break with our Canadian traditions and presents a clear and present danger to the educational programs that we cherish.

Buried in the more than 1,040 closely-spaced pages of text, annexes and schedules is a major new policy direction for education in Canada. Yet, few Canadians realize this. The federal Tory government's diligent efforts to pass off the deal as little more than the extension to Mexico of the terms of the FTA has largely succeeded: the educational community in Canada has very little sense of the Pandora's box of nasty surprises which is about to be opened on an unsuspecting public.[3]

This is partly because most of the significant changes are hidden away in the technical legalese which makes the deal largely inaccessible to those who do not make their living as international trade lawyers. It is also because the agreement is complex, with many overlapping provisions whose impact is fully realized only in the context of the overall structure of the trade deal and, more generally, in the new economic, social and political forces which are being unleashed by the deal.

Stifling Debate

The lack of information about the impact of NAFTA on education has been caused largely by the federal government carrying out the negotiations in a highly secretive manner and making virtually no effort to provide Canadians with detailed information on the various drafts of the deal during the critical period when the text was being finalized. Ironically, the little information Canadians do have about the contents of the deal came initially from 'leaked' texts released by U.S. advocacy organizations.

Unlike the final text of the FTA, which was made widely available at no cost to any Canadian who wanted a copy, and unlike the text of the Charlottetown Accord which was also widely — and freely — distributed to Canadians, the NAFTA text was not distributed in large numbers for Canadians to examine. The Tories even contracted out the right to distribute the computer software version to the private sector. For a fee of $99 (plus GST) Canadians could purchase a copy of the agreement on computer diskette from firms such as Vancouver-based Knowledge on Demand or IRL Information Retrievers Ltd.[4]

Delays in making the text available on diskette, coupled with software glitches experienced by many purchasers, meant that those who were interested in reviewing the text often had to wait months to get a copy. By that time the brief debate on NAFTA was already largely concluded. Hard copies were eventually printed, but their distribution in book stores was limited, and many Canadians are still unaware that copies can be purchased.

Restricting access to the actual text of NAFTA had the

intended effect of limiting the ability of citizens to analyze its provisions and draw their own conclusions about its content and likely effects. Instead, the government provided a range of public relations communications which lauded the benefits of the deal and maintained that it had virtually no drawbacks. Canada, we were told, came out ahead on every issue.

The government also tried to minimize the significance of the deal itself for Canada. The fact that Mexico accounts for only 2 per cent of Canada's trade was constantly repeated to support the position that NAFTA was little more than a 'housekeeping' extension of the Canada-U.S. deal to Mexico. Canadians were encouraged to think that the deal was — and would remain — quite marginal to Canada's economy and to the future of Canada's public programs. In light of this history, it is hard not to reach the conclusion that the government assumed that, in the absence of an informed debate, public opinion would be shaped by 'official' homilies about the benefits to Canada which would flow from it.

Restricting Public Input

Opportunities for citizens to voice their opinions about the deal once it became public were equally restricted. Initially, the Tories did not think it even necessary to have any hearings on the bill outside of Ottawa. After enormous public pressure was brought to bear, the House of Commons Sub-Committee on International Trade reviewing NAFTA did finally agree to hold brief sessions in five Canadian cities outside of Ontario. However, citizens in all the territories and nearly half the provinces were given no opportunity for input in their regions. Even in those provinces where hearings were held, no provision was made for citizens in outlying areas to participate. Yet despite all these restrictions, so many groups and individual citizens applied to present briefs that many were refused time for a presentation.

Both of the authors of this book were present on the second day of hearings regarding NAFTA by the Sub-Committee held in a downtown Vancouver hotel. To their astonishment, the actual text of the agreement was not given to the MPs who sat on the committee until half way through the afternoon session.

They had been given no advance copy of the 1,040-page document to study before the hearings. They had heard a full day and a half of testimony on the deal without even having a copy in front of them. Yet they were expected to evaluate the merits of the public presentations on the numerous and complex details of the agreement.

This gave the signal that the consultation process was a perfunctory exercise; a joke. No one in the government intended to revise the legislation based on the input of the public. But the charade had to be gone through because it would be too politically embarrassing to pass the legislation without any regional input at all.

After the 'consultations' were over, the Tories literally rammed NAFTA through Parliament, using closure to stifle debate and limit the opportunity of Canadians to review the text. The enabling legislation for NAFTA was 4,300 pages long. It amended 27 major acts of Parliament. Most MPs barely had time to skim the text, if they looked at it at all. The lack of opportunity for Canadians to review and study the text was pointedly noted in the final report of the Ontario Cabinet Committee on the North American Free Trade Agreement:

> Although NAFTA is a major piece of legislation that could have profound effects on Canada, the federal government has chosen not to consult the Canadian people widely about it. Public opinion in Ontario has been largely ignored. [The] (federal) House of Commons Sub-Committee on International Trade which studied NAFTA early in 1993 did not hold hearings in Ontario outside of Ottawa. The federal government invoked time allocation to limit debate on second reading of the legislation in March, 1993. The Parliamentary Committee which then studied the legislation did not hold public hearings beyond Parliament Hill. The legislation was forced through the House of Commons on May 27, 1993, and was sent to the Senate for approval.
>
> The people of Canada, and particularly of Ontario, were not given an opportunity to be heard on NAFTA.[5]

The Tory-controlled Senate — the same Senate which former Prime Minister Brian Mulroney stacked with Conservative appointees to pass the hated GST (Goods and Service, Tax) —

passed the bill on June 23, 1993, during the final week of Brian Mulroney's tenure as prime minister. Under the legislation, NAFTA can be promulgated as soon as the U.S. and Mexican governments pass it.

All this was done at the very time newly-elected U.S. President Bill Clinton was attempting to negotiate environmental and labour side-deals to the text initialled by his Republican predecessor, George Bush. The Tories fiercely opposed this initiative, arguing that there was no need to include new clauses protecting workers' rights or the environment.[6] And, in passing the bill before the issue of labour and environmental side agreements was resolved, the Tories hoped either to stifle these proposals entirely, or to minimize their scope and application.[7] They were largely successful in this effort.

Why The Unseemly Haste?

The most coherent explanation for the unseemly haste with which the Tories passed the bill at the end of their five-year mandate is quite simply that they were not prepared to allow the Canadian electorate to vote on NAFTA. They knew that most Canadians were hostile to the deal, and they feared that the electorate would reject it, as they had done the Charlottetown Accord. Therefore, they were not prepared to risk leaving the decision to a newly-elected government, with a fresh electoral mandate — a mandate which might well include a rejection of the trade deal.[8]

The general lack of concern for the views of most Canadians about NAFTA was paralleled by the lack of consultation with the organizations representing teachers, students and educational workers about the educational components of NAFTA. The Tories have made no effort to carry out an informed discussion about the possible impact of the deal for the future of education in Canada. Rather, their focus was on 'selling' the deal. In response to the questions raised by teachers at the hearings of the Sub-Committee and in response to direct enquiries, former International Trade Minister Michael Wilson sent out a letter which asserted that teachers were wrong to be at all concerned about NAFTA. However, his letter left unanswered most of the key issues raised by teachers.

Yet the impact of NAFTA is arguably of considerably greater magnitude than the proposed Charlottetown constitutional package which Canadians so agonized over. In the constitutional process, public consultations of many kinds, as well as the referendum campaign itself, allowed Canadians to make up their minds about whether they wanted to be governed under the proposed constitutional package. Canadians rejected it. Still smarting over its constitutional setback, the federal government clearly saw no benefit in allowing the details of NAFTA to be the subject of the risky process of public debate and scrutiny.

No Impact Studies On Education

As we will show in this book, NAFTA will affect public education in a number of ways — some subtle and some obvious. However, a full and comprehensive examination of how the many provisions of NAFTA will impact on education has simply not been done. Alarmingly, the federal government has released no impact studies assessing the effects of the FTA on education over the past four years. And, in the truncated and totally inadequate public hearing process carried out by the Sub-Committee on International Trade, Tory MPs indicated that none has been commissioned on NAFTA either.

The absence of impact studies is worrisome, particularly given that the federal government has already agreed to the text of the agreement and passed the legislation enabling it to be implemented. It is also worrisome because no plans appear to have been made to deal with any of the negative repercussions of the deal on Canadian education.

Canadians do have the right to know what the impact of free trade will be on educational services. Knowledge about its implications is essential in making a rational choice about whether or not to endorse the deal. The absence of impact studies and the indifference of the federal government to the possible effects on educational services indicate that the educational community has every reason to be deeply worried about what NAFTA means for education.

As a brief presented to the Ontario cabinet committee reviewing NAFTA noted:

... NAFTA contains no provisions that hold its institutional structure accountable to the citizens of Canada, the United States and Mexico. In fact, the structure is designed to minimize the inconvenience created by democratic processes.
- The disputes panels will operate under a veil of secrecy. The agreement stipulates that 'the panel's hearings, deliberations and initial report, and all written submissions to and communications with the panel shall be confidential.'
- these provisions prevent public interest groups from monitoring the panels' operations. There will be no means of knowing the kinds of information put before them and the factors taken into account in their decisions. In contrast to the principle of public access to Canadian courts and to hearings of regulatory bodies, the rules governing the operation of the dispute panels preclude even the weakest form of public accountability.
- Members of panels will be chosen from a roster of experts in law and international trade. There will be no representation of experts in other areas, despite the important consequences of panel decisions for the environment, social policy and industrial relations. With advocacy groups also shut out, the panels are likely to confine their deliberations to narrow, legal interpretations of trade issues and give precedence to the corporate rights contained in NAFTA.[9]

An unelected unaccountable international body meeting in private, will be the new arbiter, interpreting how the deal's provisions will apply to public services such as education. This process will be isolated from democratic pressures. It is difficult to see how Canada's educational community, or the broader public, will be able to have any effective input into this process.

NAFTA will affect education by changing the overall social, economic and political context in which educational decisions will be made and, more narrowly, by imposing a range of new, and quite specific, rules on the development of future educational policies and programs. These new rules are the subject of the next chapter.

Chapter Two

NAFTA: What's In The Deal?

Many of the provisions included in NAFTA will affect our system of public education indirectly. However, six chapters of the agreement will have a direct impact: Government Procurement (ch. 10); Investment (ch. 11); Cross Border Trade in Services (ch. 12); Competition Policy, Monopolies and State Enterprises (ch. 15); Intellectual Property (ch. 17) and Telecommunications (ch. 13). Perhaps the most important of these is Chapter Twelve, which covers services, and the annexes to this chapter.

The Larger Framework

Before turning to look at the provisions of specific chapters, a few comments of a more general nature are required. NAFTA must be seen not as set of discrete, independent chapters, but as the legal embodiment of a philosophical principle: let the market prevail. Certain key concepts, which we shall explain in more detail later in this chapter, are woven throughout the agreement. These include a wide variety of new 'rights', such as national treatment, for corporations and investors and a wide range of new 'rules' which will govern the policies and behaviour of governments in the future.

NAFTA's long-term — and quite explicit — objective is to

limit the ability of governments to regulate the economy, while shifting a wide range of public sector activities into the private marketplace, where they will become the basis of profit-making. The agreement views public programs as a kind of unfortunate impediment to private expansion. Under NAFTA, the value of the public sector is assessed not according to how well it meets the social, economic and cultural needs of Canadians, but rather by its contribution, or lack thereof, to the enhancement of business opportunities.

NAFTA incorporates a strong bias against pro-active government intervention in the economy and against the use of government directly to achieve public policy objectives. This is evident in its overall philosophical objectives and in many of its specific provisions.

In the preamble to the agreement, there are 15 stated goals. Only one of these even mentions the public sector. All it says is that the agreement should "preserve their ('governments') flexibility to safeguard the public welfare."[1] In the five specific objectives set out in Chapter One under Article 102: Objectives, the agreement sets out the market-oriented focus of subsequent provisions of the trade deal. These include: "eliminating barriers to trade in, and facilitate the cross-border movement of, goods and services ...", "... promot(ing) conditions of fair competition in the free trade area", "increas(ing) substantially investment opportunities in the territories of the Parties" and enforcing "intellectual property rights". There is no mention of the need to protect or preserve public programs such as public education or to ensure that governments retain the ability to manage their economies for the common good.[2]

The chapters of the deal are highly interrelated and overlapping, applying the same market principles to different areas of the economy. For example, the full implications of the chapter on services can only be understood in the context of chapters dealing with investment, government procurement, financial services and so forth. Thus companies interested in bidding on government contracts will be able to exercise 'rights' established under the investment, services, and competition policy chapters, among others.

A final introductory note about the provisions in NAFTA

affecting education must be voiced. The agreement is not static. It contains numerous provisions which require ongoing negotiations towards placing further restrictions on governments while giving corporations even more sway over a variety of economic matters which, currently, are carried out or regulated by governments. It also establishes a new and powerful international body, the Free Trade Commission, to oversee this process. Thus a process of change is institutionalized into the agreement, with target dates for meeting specific goals and with institutional structures to see that the goals are met.

NAFTA is about transforming our way of life and not merely about facilitating trade as its proponents misleadingly assert. Thus the full effects of free trade cannot be ascertained simply by reviewing the text: they must be understood in light of the economic, social and political forces which will be unleashed by the deal. We will explore these in subsequent chapters. However, in the remainder of this chapter, we shall focus more specifically on the deal itself.

Cross-Border Trade In Services

As noted above, the most important chapter in NAFTA which will impact on Canada's educational services is Chapter Twelve, the services chapter. It expands on the precedent originally negotiated in the FTA to include services in a trade agreement. (The significance of the services chapter in the FTA lay in the fact that services were not covered by the General Agreement on Tariffs and Trade (GATT) — although this may change if the current round of seemingly never-ending GATT negotiations is ever wrapped up.) The U.S. wanted not only access to the Canadian services market, but also to use the FTA as a precedent in the concurrent GATT negotiations to gain new access to service markets throughout the world.

In both the FTA and NAFTA, the services chapter opens Canada's services to U.S. companies who wish to compete in the Canadian market or to win government service contracts.

The term services encompasses a very wide range of economic activities. Broadly defined, services now include over 70 per cent of our economy. In addition to private-sector services from computing to hospitality and from management services to fast foods, it also sweeps in a large part of the public sector, including education, under its broadly-defined provisions. (There are exceptions, which we will discuss in a moment.)

It sets the framework within which governments in future will deal with services transactions. This is a 'commercial' or business framework. It is within this commercial framework that public and, specifically, educational services are covered. This is a major change because Canada's history has been one of viewing public services as a separate, non-commercial sector which operates according to a different set of values.

Although Canada's private educational services sector is considerably smaller, proportionately, than that of the U.S., it is still substantial. There are private language centres, private training academies, and private trades schools. And there are private colleges offering a wide range of certificates, diplomas and other competency affirmations such as accounting, business administration, bookkeeping, computer programming, real estate, food services management and preparation, hotel management, auto mechanics, welding, electronics repairs and a host of other skills.

There have been private night-school and correspondence courses for generations, but in recent years the development of new technology has opened the door to a wide range of new private educational services. Cable television, video, computer communications and a host of new interactive communications systems make it possible for private firms to offer a much larger range of programs and services. And the private sector is intent on expanding this market.

Not only does Canada already have a substantial commercial educational sector, but one in which there is no clear-cut boundary between many of the services offered by private firms and our public educational institutions. Nor is there any clear-cut funding division. A number of private educational services receive all, or a substantial part, of their enrolment fees from government. In some cases, such as federal training programs, they compete directly with public institutions such as community colleges for students. Instead of being two distinct sectors, public and private educational services overlap and often compete. This reality should be borne in mind in conceptualizing the impact of the services chapter of NAFTA on Canada's educational system.

The Mandate Of The Services Chapter

Article 1201: Scope and Coverage sets out the mandate of the services chapter. It is a very sweeping mandate, applying to:

a) the production, distribution, marketing, sale and delivery of a service;

b) the purchase or use of, or payment for, a service;

c) the access to and use of distribution and transportation systems in connection with provisions of a service;

d) the presence in its territory of a service provider of another Party;

e) the provision of a bond or other form of financial security as a condition for the provision of a service.

The remainder of the article sets out certain exceptions to this broad mandate, a number of which (financial services and government procurement) are actually dealt with in a slightly different fashion in other parts of the agreement. Article 1201 also makes reference to the application of the services chapter to public programs and services. Under the third and last subsection, it says:

3. Nothing in this Chapter shall be construed to:

b) prevent a Party from providing a service or performing a function, such as law enforcement, correctional services, income security or insurance, social security or insurance, social welfare, public education, public training, health, and child care, in a manner that is not inconsistent with this Chapter.

Cutting though the clause's double negatives (which would have any English teacher slashing with a red pen), the agreement allows governments to continue to run public education systems — but within the rules set out in Chapter Twevle. It is precisely these commercial rules that present a danger to what most Canadians value about our system of public education.

No Preference To Canadian Firms

Chapter Twelve is based on two key concepts introduced in the FTA. They are both borrowed from international trade agreements which formerly applied only to goods. These are: (1) the concept of 'national treatment' and (2) the 'right of establishment'.

National treatment gives U.S. firms all the rights and privileges of domestic Canadian firms. In other words, government policy must treat U.S. firms (and Mexican, under NAFTA) as if they were Canadian. The right of establishment — which is set out more fully in the FTA — requires Canadian governments to get rid of all policies which restrict U.S. firms from setting up in Canada or which limit tendering on public contracts to established Canadian firms.

The provision on national treatment is found in Article 1202 and reads as follows:

1. Each Party shall accord to service providers of another Party treatment no less favourable than it accords, in like circumstances, to its own service providers.

2. The treatment accorded by a Party under paragraph 1 means, with respect to a state or province, treatment no less favourable than the most favourable treatment accorded, in like circumstances, by that state or province to service providers of the Party of which it forms a part.[3]

This provision requires Canadian governments to give U.S. and Mexican service firms the same rights and privileges as Canadian service providers. In other words, governments are prevented from exercising policies which would favour Canadian service firms.[4]

No Local Presence

NAFTA greatly expands the rights of national treatment and right of establishment given to U.S. service firms under section 1402 of the FTA. Not only must Canada ensure that U.S. firms are permitted to set up or 'establish' in Canada under exactly the same rules as Canadian firms, NAFTA also prevents Canadian governments from requiring that such companies even have a "local presence" in Canada. Article 1205:

Local Presence states:

> No Party may require a service provider of another Party to establish or maintain a representative office or any form of enterprise, or to be resident, in its territory as a condition for the cross-border provision of a service.[5]

U.S. companies can thus carry out work or services in Canada without having any investment in the country, without providing any employment and without even having an office in Canada. In an era of faxes, modems and high-tech telecommunications, foreign firms will be increasingly able to take advantage of such 'rights'.

These provisions signal the end of long-standing practices by governments in Canada giving preference to domestic or, in the case of provincial governments, to provincial or locally-based service suppliers. It abolishes practices designed to limit access to the Canadian market, such as requiring a special domestic licence or having a local office as conditions for offering educational services to Canadian students. In short, large U.S. service firms are being given full access to the Canadian services market.

The principles of national treatment and right of establishment, when combined with the bar against governments requiring a local presence, gives U.S. companies unfettered rights to compete for Canadian students purchasing private courses. The federal and provincial governments could not attempt to reserve such courses for Canadian firms, as this would violate NAFTA's principles.

Opening Up Canada To U.S. Multinationals

What are some of the implications of these new rules? In the context of a hemispheric market where pre-packaged educational and training modules can be mass-marketed, Canadian firms will find themselves at a very severe disadvantage because they do not have the economies of scale, or a sufficiently large market to compete with well-established U.S. firms. To the extent that the U.S. firms could handle some of their data processing and administrative work in low-wage jurisdictions, Canadian firms would be even more hardpressed.

Another implication, as noted above, is that public licensing and regulation of educational service providers would have to be carried out in a manner which did not favour domestic firms. Certain Canadian practices and standards might well be viewed as 'protectionist' and therefore open to challenge by U.S. firms who felt their 'rights' were violated.

But there is a very important distinction between Canada and Mexico under NAFTA on this matter. Mexico insisted — and got — a lengthy and very specific exemption to the services chapter, allowing it virtually total control over all aspects of private education in Mexico.

The Mexican Annex V to NAFTA includes specific provisions dealing with private educational services at all levels. These services are clearly set out by industry sub-sector so that the extent of state regulation can be defined and grandparented. That is to say, existing practices would be protected. The industry classifications are as follows:

Sector: Private Educational Services

Sub Sector: (none listed)

Industry Classification:

CMAP 921101 — Private Preschool Educational Services

CMAP 921102 — Private Primary School Educational Services

CMAP 921103 — Private Secondary School Educational Services

CMAP 921104 — Private Middle High (Prepatory) School Educational Services

CMAP 921105 — Private Higher School Educational Services

CMAP 921106 — Private Educational Services that combine Preschool, Primary, Secondary, Middle High and Higher School Instruction

Level of Government: Federal and State

The Mexican Annex then proceeds to list the various pieces of legislation and public regulation which currently apply to private educational institutions. The description of these is as follows:

For the provision of primary, secondary, 'normal' or worker or peasant educational services, prior and express authorization granted by the Secretaria de Educacion Publica or the state competent authority is required. Such authorization is granted or cancelled on a case-by-case basis in accordance with public convenience and necessity, at the discretion of the Secretaria de Educacion Publica or the state competent authority. No legal remedy is available under Mexican law for the denial or revocation of such authorization.

In this annex, Mexico has clarified the continuing right of its government to regulate private schools. Not so for Canada. Its section of the same annex says nothing. There is no 'grandparenting' of the regulatory capacity of federal and provincial governments with respect to private schools. There is no attempt to assert the right of government to regulate in this area.

The presumption which follows from this is that private educational institutions operating in Canada, but owned in the U.S., would have the same rights as other commercial enterprises, namely national treatment, right of establishment and so forth.

The abandonment by governments in Canada of their authority to regulate private educational services raises questions about how Canadian content could be protected. There will be enormous pressure for Canadian governments to accept the practice of U.S. firms offering U.S. educational modules produced for a U.S. audience through branch operations in Canada. The examples and illustrations in such educational material are very unlikely to reflect the Canadian experience or Canadian practices. Yet, if federal or provincial governments try to impose domestic course-content requirements they will have to evaluate and monitor *all* the programs which are being offered by firms engaged in cross-border services trade. This is highly impractical and therefore highly unlikely.

The 'local presence' provision also has implications for employment. U.S. firms offering services in Canada through computer and cable hook-ups are permitted to do so without using Canadian staff. Interactive technology will make it possible for an instructor in Dallas or Atlanta to deal with a student in Saskatchewan entirely through telecommunications links. No Canadians need be involved in the instructional process at all.

Already this is beginning to happen on a large scale. New York University, for example, offers courses to Canadians for degrees by correspondence. Other U.S. universities have similar programs. Some of these go back a number of years, but their role was always relatively minor. NAFTA will change this dramatically, especially as the private, profit-driven colleges realize that they have all the rights of Canadian firms in soliciting students in the Canadian market.

Another concern arises from the fact that more and more educational services which, historically, have been carried out in the public sector are being privatized. This is happening either through direct transfer to the private sector or as a result of public institutions withdrawing due to fiscal constraints. Consequently, as a larger share of Canada's overall education spending is channelled through the private sector, as U.S. firms exercise their rights under NAFTA, more and more of Canada's education system will become 'Americanized'. This will occur both as U.S. firms market existing programs in Canada and as they exercise the right to buy out Canadian educational firms (under the investment provisions which we shall deal with later). By analogy, private control of cable television has led to almost total U.S. dominance of the programs shown and a step-by-step retreat by the Canadian Radio-television and Telecommunications Commission (CRTC) from requiring any significant level of Canadian content.

Under NAFTA, it will not be possible for governments to resist this trend toward Americanization, for the tools needed to impose Canadian standards and regulations are denied by the deal.

An Example From B.C.

Let's look at another example of the way governments will lose control. In British Columbia, Grade 12 provincial examinations certify that students have met the requirements for graduation.

Preparation of Grade 12 examinations is currently contracted out by the B.C. government to a locally-based firm. However, when this contract is re-tendered, it could well be the subject of international bidding.

To prepare these examinations properly, a contractor would have to have much more than a comprehensive knowledge of the subject matter. The contractor would also have to know about the cultural elements reflected in the curriculum and practices of the schools — cultural elements that are seldom explicitly stated, but are still of fundamental significance.

Because NAFTA recognizes services only as an economic commodity, the B.C. government would be obligated to let American contractors bid on an equal basis with B.C. contractors.[6] (Theoretically, Mexican contractors could bid on the contract as well, but this is far less likely for linguistic and institutional reasons.)

Efforts by provincial governments, such as B.C.'s, to ensure that the distinctive culture and traditions of its school system are reflected in the contract tenders could face a bid challenge from U.S. firms under the new NAFTA rules. U.S. firms could credibly claim that these cultural elements are nothing more than an attempt to give preference to local firms (i.e., to erect a non-tariff barrier). The province would have to justify its tendering process and could be forced to change it to accommodate U.S. demands.

Chapter Twelve will also impact on a wide range of support services such as cleaning, food services, school bus transportation, building maintenance, computer services, consulting, temporary office help and the like. Any of these which are carried out directly by the ministries of education of the various provinces will eventually be covered.

Unlike the services chapter of the FTA, NAFTA contains a number of references to 'local government'. Local government includes school boards. The references are to indicate that local government practices are not (yet) governed by the services chapter of the NAFTA.

However, given the way NAFTA has dramatically expanded the scope of the FTA and given the fact that NAFTA sets up an ongoing process of continuous review with the explicit purpose of expanding the market principles at the core of the agreement, there is no reason to believe that local governments will remain exempt permanently, or indeed even for very long.

A future decision, made with little or no consultation by the increasingly powerful Free Trade Commission and its Secretariat, with the tacit agreement of our federal government, could quietly sweep local governments into the deal, with profound implications for school boards across the country.

In Canada, local governments are creatures of the provinces. They have no distinct constitutional status. Their scope and mandate, as well as boundaries and financing, can be altered by acts of the respective provincial legislatures. In some provinces, public education at the primary and secondary levels is already highly centralized, with matters such as salaries and budgets controlled by the provincial government, rather than the local school board. Consequently, where a province is directly involved in administering contracts for educational supplies and services, a strong case can be made that the trade deal will be directly applicable.

However, the distinction between provincial and local levels of government may be misleading. Local levels of government are heavily dependent on provincial financing. Since the local governments are also the creatures of provincial legislation, provinces could be pressured to issue regulations requiring them to adhere to the principles of the deal as well. Indeed, the real question is not whether, but how long it will take for these levels of government to be fully covered.

Servicing McDonald's

Food services in primary and secondary schools may well be opened up to bidding by large multinational firms like Burger King and McDonald's. With universities, the practice of contracting out such services is already pervasive. The NAFTA will simply entrench the right of U.S. companies to bid on these contracts.

In Ontario there has been a major push by the U.S. firm Servicemaster to take over the management of custodial and maintenance services. The company has acquired a number of contracts with southwestern Ontario school boards and is attempting to expand its activities across the province. The management of certain health and social services is already covered by the FTA, and educational services are a logical next step.

Once having obtained a contract to manage the service, the firm has moved quickly to put in place its own arrangements for purchasing supplies and equipment. It has also reorganized the operations and working practices of the custodians and other employees under its direction. Its U.S.-style labour relations practices have been the subject of criticism by the union representing the workers in a number of the schools it has taken over. But more importantly, it is not self-evident that the expansion of the role of multinational firms in such educational service areas will contribute to the development of the kind of school community which many teachers and parents wish to preserve.

Making Reservations An Inexact Science

Those familiar with the text of NAFTA may say "ah, but you exaggerate the potential dangers because you have missed the protections outlined in the Article 1206 on reservations." This article reads as follows:

1. Articles 1202, 1203 and 1205 do not apply to:
    a) any existing non-conforming measure that is maintained by
        i) a Party at the federal level, as set out in its Schedule to Annex I,
        ii) a state or province, for two years after the date of entry into force of this Agreement, and thereafter as set out by a Party in its Schedule to Annex I in accordance with paragraph 2, or
        iii) a local government
    b) the continuation or prompt renewal of any non-conforming measure referred to in subparagraph (a); or
    c) an amendment to any non-conforming measure referred to in subparagraph (a) to the extent that the amendment does not decrease the conformity of the measure, as it existed immediately before the amendment, with Articles 1202, 1203 and 1205.
2. Each Party may set out in its Schedule to Annex I, within two years of the date of entry into force of this Agreement,

any existing non-conforming measure maintained by a state or province, not including a local government.

3. Articles 1202, 1203 and 1205 do not apply to any measure that a Party adopts or maintains with respect to sectors, sub-sectors or activities, as set out in its Schedule to Annex II.

On the surface, Article 1206 allows for a province to exclude "existing" services from open competition from U.S. educational contractors. Under the social services sector of Annex ll of NAFTA, referred to above, Canada reserves the right to be exempted from five components of the trade deal: National Treatment (Articles 1102, 1202), Most Favoured Nation Treatment (Article 1203), Local Presence (Article 1205) and Senior Management and Boards of Directors (Article 1107).

The Description of this reservation is as follows:

Cross-Border Services and Investment

Canada reserves the right to adopt or maintain any measure with respect to the provision of public law enforcement and correctional services, and the following services to the extent that they are social services established or maintained for a public purpose: income security or insurance, social security or insurance, social welfare, public education, public training, health, and child care.

There are several points to be made about this exemption. First, it is conditional on the services being "established or maintained for a public purpose," an expression whose meaning is open to legal interpretation.

Second, the question of what is actually included under the categories "public education", "public training" or "child care" is also subject to interpretation. Does the definition of public education exclude public regulation of 'private education'? How is the boundary between public and private educational services to be determined, especially when there is already a substantial overlap?

Third, it is notable that the qualifications included in this 'exemption' are not included in the exemption dealing with aboriginal affairs. Its provision is very clear: "Canada reserves the right to adopt or maintain any measure denying investors of another Party and their investments, or service providers of another Party, any rights or preferences provided to aboriginal peoples." Why is the wording of the educational exemption so much weaker?

Restrictions On New Services

Several other limitations apply to the right to exempt particular services from competition by U.S. service providers on the same basis as Canadian firms.

The first limitation is the ability of governments to designate only "existing" services as exempt. Thus, all new educational services — in principle at least — cannot be included under the exemptions listed under Article 1206. They must be open to transnational competition. The point of this provision is to stop the expansion of government regulations or public programs. It is to provide a 'ceiling' on an future expansion of government.

Constricting Daycare

As an example, if the federal government were ever to live up to its 1988 election promise of a national daycare program, it would run into conflict with the deal if it tried to specify that the program must be a publicly administered and staffed program, or even that it be run only by Canadian non-profit organizations (thus excluding U.S. for-profit daycare operations).

Because a national, publicly-funded and publicly-staffed daycare program would be a new government service, the Canadian government would be required to consult with the other governments under Articles 1804: Administrative Proceedings; 1805: Review and Appeal and 2006: Consultations. This latter article is a 'catch-all' provision which gives each government the right to ask the Free Trade Commission to review any measure it feels could negatively affect its rights or the rights of its companies under NAFTA. Moreover, Article 2004: Nullification and Impairment specifically names the services chapter as one which qualifies for recourse to the dispute settlement provisions of Chapter Twenty. It reads:

> 1. If any Party considers that any benefit it could reasonably have expected to accrue to it under any provision of:

... (c) Chapter Twelve (Cross Border Trade in Services) ... is being nullified or impaired as a result of the application of any measure that is not inconsistent with this agreement, the Party may have recourse to dispute settlement under this Chapter.

Most Canadians think of services such as daycare as small-scale operations. Public daycare is normally administered by individual municipalities, school boards or provincially-controlled public agencies. Non-profit daycare is administered by local community boards controlled by parents and community activists. Even private, for-profit daycare is still small-scale in most areas. Most is in the form of home-based 'family daycare' run by individuals. And the commercial operations — which many daycare advocates strongly oppose — do not dominate the daycare sector.

However, there are a significant number of for-profit commercial daycare firms operating in Canada. Some of these are owned by large U.S. daycare chains. But compared with the U.S., the Canadian market is relatively 'undeveloped'. Perhaps a better adjective would be unexploited.

In the U.S., daycare, a commercial service, is also big business. Private daycare firms operate on a totally different scale than in Canada. To cite just one illustration, the *Globe and Mail* business section recently reported the acquisition of Petite Academy Inc., a U.S. company traded on the New York Stock Exchange, by Vestar Capital Partners Ltd. Vestar and a group of Petite's managers agreed to pay $170 million for the outstanding shares of Petite. In 1992, Petite had revenues of $245 million from operations spanning 33 U.S. states. Its 780 daycare centres provide spaces for 83,000 children.[7]

There are numerous other large U.S. commercial daycare operators who see this service as an expanding market for profitable investment. And the political culture in the U.S. is much more favourably inclined to commercial, for-profit daycare operations than in Canada. In a society which believes that government is inherently bad and that business can do almost everything more efficiently, the expansion of commercial daycare operators to fill the void left by an inadequately funded public educational system is viewed with favour. And, the negotiation of new rights and protections for commercial service providers in the FTA and NAFTA is seen as a simple extension of existing U.S. practices to the international level.

Compensating Business For Daycare

Under NAFTA, a future Canadian government committed to establishing a new, publicly-administered national daycare program could be required to pay U.S. firms compensation for the resulting loss of market opportunities once these companies had established a significant presence in the Canadian market. This is because providing daycare directly through the public sector would clearly limit the ability of private firms to continue to operate, or to expand, their profit-making activities in this area.

The basis for calculating the extent of these lost-profit opportunities would be the daycare firms' projections of potential profits over the following decades. While the exact amounts would vary according to a number of assumptions (and we can be sure that the corporate lawyers and accountants would be busy developing the most inflated case), it is clear that the intention is to make the level of compensation very favourable to the firms involved. This would act as an effective deterrent to the creation of new public programs.

Moreover, whatever compensation had to be paid to these firms would have to be matched by similar compensation to Canadian private sector daycare operators. Otherwise they could claim discrimination.

All this means that before a single new public or non-profit daycare space could be opened up, the government would have to pay out massive compensation to private firms. No daycare services would flow from this compensation: it would only be to fulfil the terms of NAFTA. Truly, this is a major intrusion on Canadian education policy. It may also explain why the Mulroney government quietly shelved its much-touted 1988 election commitment to set up a national daycare program.

To those who think this scenario far-fetched, one only needs to point to the 1991 decision by the Ontario government to renege on its commitment to enact public auto insurance.

Threats by the international insurance industry, backed up by calculations of billions of dollars in compensation for the loss of the Ontario market, were sufficient to force a newly-elected — and perhaps overly timid — New Democratic Party (NDP) government to back down from the most high-profile campaign commitment it had made during the 1990 election.

Once the current federal Tory government has left office, a new government will be required to honour the terms of the treaty. The U.S. will not be concerned about whether Canadian citizens were properly informed about the implications of NAFTA. Nor will the U.S. be interested in hearing Canadians complain that they were misled by the Mulroney/Campbell Tory government. It will simply point out that we have a legally binding treaty to honour.

A basic problem that any future government will also have in dealing with this issue is that, however unreasonable the provision is with respect to national programs such as daycare, the only way to avoid paying compensation would be to abrogate the entire agreement. The drafters of NAFTA have calculated that abrogation would be such an enormous step, affecting so many other areas of the economy, that no government would be prepared to do so simply to get rid of the limitations imposed on a new public program such as daycare. Hence future governments will simply concede to corporate demands and abandon any commitments they may make with respect to a national child-care program, or other new public educational services.

Another point arising from this example is that the *expectations* of U.S. firms have been profoundly changed by free trade. These firms are being encouraged to believe that they now have the right to full and free access to Canada's markets, where they will be permitted to operate just as they do in the U.S. Thus they will see public-sector provision of any new service as a denial of their rights under the deal — a perception which would not exist if Canada had not embarked on the path of free trade.

Existing Services Not Properly Protected

A second limitation of the reservations provision of the services chapter is that under Article 1206, section 1, subsection

(a) number (ii) cited above, a provincial government must — within two years — designate existing services as being exempt from the national treatment, right of establishment and local presence provisions. Any service not specifically designated will, after two years, automatically fall into the 'open for transnational competition' category.

This designation process itself contains a strong anti-public service bias. As any labour negotiator knows, the best kind of collective agreement clause is one which gives your side all the rights except those specifically listed as exceptions granted to the other side. Thus if something has been forgotten, or if a new issue arises, you are automatically entitled to it because it is not listed as belonging to the other side. This is precisely how the services chapter deals with the public sector. If it's not listed among the exemptions, then it is automatically covered.

Provincial governments may well fail to list certain services, either through oversight (because there is no comprehensive list for guidance) or because they wish to see them eventually privatized and the trade deal provides a convenient way to facilitate this. Not all provincial governments may want the same services excluded: hence there will be pressure to accept the lowest common denominator. And, finally, the federal government, which has the power to do the listing, will be in a very strong position to force provinces to leave out some services in exchange for inclusion of others (or as part of a larger federal-provincial trade-off).

The Ratchet Effect

The most serious limitation, though, on the ability of Canadians to protect and improve the educational and social services they value is what University of Toronto professor David Clandfield has described as the "ratchet effect." In an article on the original FTA in *Our School/Our Selves* (Vol. 4, No. 2, pp. 198), he quoted from the Gage Canadian Dictionary the definition of ratchet:

> a wheel or bar with teeth that strike against a catch fixed so that motion is permitted in one direction by not in another.

The "ratchet effect" of NAFTA is "a mechanism that allows

the wheel of government action to move in one direction only and never to reverse." Initially, protected government services can become open to trans-border bidding, but government can never move those services back to the protected category.

Where are these 'ratchet' mechanisms in NAFTA?

One is in the already mentioned limitation that only services listed under the 'exclusion' schedules will be exempted from the disciplines of the trade deal.

A second comes in Article 1206, section 1.(c), which allows amendments to existing programs only if "the amendment does not decrease the conformity" of the program to the trinational competition provisions. As an example, once the B.C. government made the creation of Grade 12 exams open to contract competition, it could not bring the writing of the exams back inside the Ministry of Education without facing a challenge — even if it discovered the task could be better performed only by teachers with B.C. experience who worked directly for the provincial government.

The bar of the ratchet is the provision in Article 1209: Procedures that requires "(b) consultations on reservations, quantitative restrictions or commitments with a view to further liberalization." These consultations on reservations are to be supervised by the newly-established Free Trade Commission, which will also be in charge of the listing process.

The agreement thus commits the three governments to review and renegotiate the so called "non-conforming measures." Nothing that is currently exempt is permanently exempt. Indeed, the very way in which NAFTA is framed means that many of the cherished, and successful, Canadian ways of providing services are treated as anomalies or inconsistencies which eventually will have to be harmonized out of existence. This is the only inference one can draw from the use of the term 'non-conforming' to describe our public approach to providing educational services.

The ratchet can go only one way — towards making all services into commodities, open to competition from service providers in all three countries. Attempts to go in the opposite direction — returning them to the public sector — are blocked by unreasonable and deliberately punitive penalties.

In taking back a privatized service, according to the twisted logic of the deal, governments would be excluding private business from a profitable market. Consequently, firms must be given compensation for this loss of opportunity. Faced with the hassle and cost of fighting to bring a service back 'in house' — not to speak of the lobbying from business interests — many provincial governments will simply throw in the towel and keep contracting out, even if they believe it is not the best way to provide the service.

As we noted earlier, one form of penalty is a requirement that American companies be financially compensated for the loss of the right to operate a service. Another penalty provision allows retaliation by the country whose companies are excluded from providing services. Thus, an attempt by the B.C. government to bring the creation of Grade 12 exams back into direct government service could lead to penalties on a B.C. export, such as lumber.

Harmonization Of Professional Standards

The existing FTA section on the provision of cross-border professional services and certification requirements has been greatly expanded in NAFTA, with major implications for educational workers.

Section A.1 of Annex 1210 states that: "This annex applies to measures adopted or maintained by a Party relating to the licensing and certification of professional service providers."

The definition of "professional services" appears to apply to primary and secondary school teachers as well as a range of other professionals currently teaching at various public educational institutions. Article 1213 defines professional services as:

> services, the provision of which requires specialized post-secondary education, or equivalent training or experience, and for which the right to practice is granted or restricted by measures adopted or maintained by a Party.

Across Canada, provincial governments either directly issue certificates providing the right to teach, or else authorize a 'college' to grant certificates. The basis of granting certificates to teachers varies from one jurisdiction to another, reflecting different social experiences and education philosophies. However, in all cases it reflects a concern by the public to maintain democratic control over the educational system.

In Canada, the implicit philosophy behind certification in most provinces has been one of teachers receiving a broad education in pedagogical processes after a general arts and science education as an undergraduate student. This combination of broad education in subject matter and pedagogical methods provides a basis for the teacher to learn and adjust to teaching in particular subject areas, and to acquire knowledge on an ongoing basis throughout her/his career as both the teaching assignment and the knowledge base in the area being taught evolves and develops.

In other words, from the general preparation as a teacher, the authorities who grant a certificate expect teaching professionals to maintain and improve their capacity to teach in an education system that is constantly evolving to reflect changes in social conditions and the growing base of knowledge. In most provinces, changes in the programs and curriculum of the schools are centrally determined through the provincial ministry of education and the cabinet and not left primarily to local school boards or individual teachers to determine.

How The U.S. Differs

Most American states have a very different philosophical approach. While they have less government determination of programs and curriculum, they have much more specialized certification of teachers. Rather than general certification such as we have here, a teacher in most states is certified for teaching only in particular subjects and grade levels. Specific formal, course-based upgrading is frequently a requirement of maintaining a certificate.

The point here is not to argue that one is better than the other, but that they are significantly different. The differences reflect the fact that certification of teachers is imbedded within complex cultural practices that make up education. Because of that, they are not easily changed, nor should they be.

But because NAFTA is based on a view that sees education and all other services as primarily economic exchanges, it demands negotiation to harmonize the practices in each of the countries.

Specifically, Annex 1210 calls for "development of mutually acceptable professional standards and criteria." The areas defined for common standards include "conduct and ethics, professional development and re-certification and scope of practice." It is in these areas, as indicated above, that there are differences between what generally applies in Canada and in the United States.

The bodies that certify professionals are "to provide recommendations on mutual recognition to the (Free Trade) Commission." The commission then "shall review the recommendations within a reasonable period to determine whether they are consistent with this Agreement. Based upon the Commission's review, the Parties shall encourage their respective competent authorities, where appropriate, to adopt these recommendations within a mutually agreed period."

This is an entirely unwarranted and inappropriate interference in an area which has been seen as important from a social and cultural, as well as pedagogical, perspective. The commitment to review the process of certification for various professionals — with the intention of harmonizing standards within the free trade area — constitutes a major intrusion into the historic, constitutional powers of provincial governments. This section of NAFTA may eventually see an international commission asserting powers over education that are not granted to the federal government in Canada's Constitution.

It has taken place without consultation with teachers and most other professional associations. The federal government appears to have decided to downplay these commitments to minimize opposition before the deal is locked into place. However, this 'railroading' of a commitment within NAFTA to develop new certification procedures can only raise further concerns about the kind of 'consultation' which will occur when the details of the standards are being determined by the Free Trade Commission.

It is reasonable to ask why the negotiators included these provisions in NAFTA. Certainly, there is no popular pressure in Canada for these measures. The vast majority of teachers do not even know about them. Yet once implemented, NAFTA will begin a process of consultation and standard setting whose outcome is already pre-determined, regardless of whether this is seen as advantageous or harmful to education in Canada.

While the issue of teacher certification was barely raised before the Canadian parliament passed NAFTA, it is now being taken seriously by educators who support the deal in the U.S. and Mexico. Interest in harmonization of certification is most pronounced in the states along the U.S.-Mexico border. In a document prepared in March, 1992 by the School of Education, University of Southern California, the desirability of establishing common standards of certification, not only for teachers but also with respect to educational standards in the three countries, is clearly stated:

> A tri-national commission should consider how the three North American countries will determine fitness to work or provide services. The establishment of a common set of education standards could be formally enforced through a certification system acceptable to all three partners.[8]

The University of Southern California proposal included the creation of a powerful trilateral education commission to oversee the work of harmonizing educational programs, standards and certification. Such initiatives remain at the proposal stage, but once the deal is ratified by all three countries they will be given an enormous impetus.

While this may still seem remote — indeed far-fetched — to most Canadians, the pattern of tri-national educational harmonization will be driven at an increasing speed by the U.S. and Mexico, as the deal locks into place. Canada will end up simply being pulled along to conform with the requirements of the deal itself and to avoid being totally excluded from decisions which will shape hemispheric integration.

Government Procurement

Another key chapter in the FTA which has been expanded in NAFTA is the one dealing with public purchasing or government procurement, Chapter Ten. This chapter is important because in many ways it overlaps, and supplements, the services chapter in guaranteeing new rights to U.S. (and Mexican) firms. As with the services chapter, the principle of national treatment is paramount. Basically, each of the signatory governments agrees that it will treat companies based in the other countries in a manner similar to their own companies in the tendering and awarding of government contracts, including service contracts. As with the services chapter, there is no requirement that they have a physical 'presence' in the jurisdiction where they are bidding on contracts.

The initial application of this chapter varies according to the level of government, with the federal government immediately committing itself to specific thresholds for contracts for goods and services of $50,000 and $6.5 million (US) for construction contracts. (The lower FTA thresholds are 'grandparented' for U.S. firms.) NAFTA also brings federal Crown corporations under the scope of its procurement provisions, thus expanding beyond the requirements of the FTA. Federal Crown corporations have a higher threshold of $250,000 for goods and services and $8 million (US) for construction contracts.[9]

Provincial, state and local governments and their enterprises and agencies are not immediately covered. However, Article 1024 commits Canada to a process of negotiation which is intended to bring these levels of government under the rules of the chapter. It reads as follows:

1. The Parties shall commence further negotiations no later than December 31, 1998, with a view to the further liberalization of their respective government procurement markets.

2. In such negotiations, the Parties shall review all aspects of their government procurement practices for purposes of:
    a) assessing the functioning of their government procurement systems;
    b) seeking to expand the coverage of this Chapter, including by adding
       (i) other government enterprises, and
       (ii) procurement otherwise subject to legislated or administrative exceptions; and
    c) reviewing thresholds.

3. Prior to such review, the Parties shall endeavour to consult with their state and provincial governments with a view to obtaining commitments, on a voluntary and reciprocal basis, to include within this chapter procurement by state and provincial government entities and enterprises.[10]

Thus, while initially the rules will apply only to federal purchases, as the above provisions indicate, the long-term (and it is not that long) intention is to require provincial and perhaps even local governments to follow the same procedures. Provincial Crown corporations and agencies will be the subject of further negotiations as well.

The NAFTA commitment to eventually include other levels of government and their enterprises was not part of the FTA. It constitutes a major new commitment by Canada, limiting the ability of future governments to use public procurement as an economic and social policy tool.

Section C, Article 1017: Bid Challenge, provides a very detailed process for allowing U.S. and Mexican companies to appeal procurement decisions which they feel have not given them full and fair consideration. Essentially, the onus is on the government to prove that it has not violated the 'rights' of the foreign firm. To facilitate this process, each government must establish an impartial reviewing authority to investigate the bid challenge. This authority must have the right to delay the awarding of the contract or to require that it be re-tendered. It can also demand that the government change its tendering procedures to "... bring them into conformity with this Chapter."

Giving Multinationals The Edge

As a result of these new rules, large multinational consulting and educational services firms will have enormous advantages in bidding on public contracts. Unlike many local suppliers and contractors, the large firms will have the benefits of volume, scale of operations, sophisticated public relations and marketing and the ability to develop packages of materials which can be used across North America. The standardized tendering requirements will also make it much easier for them to submit bids as they will not have to shape their proposals to the specific requirements of each country's (or state or province's) tendering system.

The procurement chapter will guarantee U.S. firms full access to government educational purchases of computers, supplies, teaching aids and a wide range of educational equipment.

As we noted in our discussion in the services chapter, there has been a sharp increase in the activity of U.S.-based service firms such as Marriott and Servicemaster. The new rules on procurement, once they extend to provincial and local governments, would enable such firms to challenge public decisions intended to return certain services to the public sector from two directions: violations of their 'rights' under the services chapter and violations of the procurement provisions. Because of the greater specificity of the procurement chapter's bid challenge procedures, disputes over matters such as terminating a privatized service may well be raised under the provisions of this chapter.

The procurement chapter may also have significant implications in areas such as textbook purchases. While Canadian history texts will likely not be subject to bidding from U.S. publishing and supply firms, areas such as science, language, mathematics, computing and many others could be opened up to international tendering.

No one would question the fact that in these subjects there are very good texts produced by U.S., British and other publishers. But the point is whether it is appropriate for Canadian ministries of education to be required to adopt a new tendering process to ensure that U.S. publishers are given full rights to bid on textbook contracts in Canadian schools. This might be acceptable if the goal were to integrate Canada into the United States. But for the purpose of protecting our educational traditions, giving priority to a McDonald's-type approach to tendering for educational services is unlikely to provide the outcome most Canadians desire.

Investment In Education

On the face of it, it may seem peculiar to view the investment provisions of a trade deal as having any implications for public services such as education. However, the investment chapter, Chapter Eleven, does make reference to public services in a manner which parallels the language in the services chapter.

Under Article 1101: Scope and Coverage, it states:

4. Nothing in this Chapter shall be construed to prevent a Party from providing a service or performing a function such as law enforcement, correctional services, income security or insurance, social security or insurance, social welfare, public education, public training, health, and child care, in a manner that is not inconsistent with this Chapter.

As with the services chapter, the proviso "in a manner that is not inconsistent with this Chapter" gives rise to basic questions about what it means not to be in conflict with the other provisions of the investment chapter.

The investment chapter includes the commitment to national treatment found in other chapters. It guarantees that U.S. and Mexican investors will be treated in the same way as Canadian investors by federal and provincial governments, and it forbids requirements that certain enterprises must have a specified level of investment held by Canadians (Article 1002, subsection 4).

Thus, for example, provincial governments could not require that educational service suppliers be majority-owned by Canadians.

The investment chapter contains a wide range of provisions which limit how governments can deal with U.S. or Mexican investors. One of the key new restrictions deals with the expropriation of investors. Article 1110: Expropriation and Compensation reads as follows:

1. No party may directly or indirectly nationalize or expropriate an investment of an investor of another Party in its territory or take a measure tantamount to nationalization or expropriation of such an investment ("Expropriation"), except:
    a) for a public purpose;
    b) on a non-discriminatory basis;
    c) in accordance with due process of law and Article 1105(1); and
    d) on payment of compensation in accordance with paragraphs 2 through 6.

The payment provisions require immediate payment at 'fair

market value' and the right of the investor to be paid in a currency which can immediately be repatriated to the investor's home country.

What is significant about the investment provisions of the deal is that they severely restrict the ability of governments to set up new public programs in areas where private companies now operate. Investors will have the right to take their claim for compensation to an international arbitration tribunal, the International Centre for Settlement of Investment Disputes. Thus federal or provincial governments will lose the right to legislate the terms upon which they compensate private investors for the takeover of their operations or for the elimination of their access to a service 'market'.

The question of what constitutes a "public purpose" also arises in this chapter. Certainly the definition is open to a number of interpretations. What may be seen as a legitimate public purpose in Canada may, from a U.S. perspective be viewed as a totally unwarranted intrusion by government into the private market. Moreover, if the arbitration panel decides that the expropriation was not for a suitable "public purpose", it has the right under Article 1135: Final Award to insist on the "restitution of property" which presumably would entail the right to continue to operate in the area previously expropriated.

The punitive provisions of the investment chapter would, for example, make it difficult for a new federal government to take back the training contracts which are now being handed out to a variety of private, profit-making training companies. It reinforces Clandfield's ratchet effect, discussed under the services chapter, and provides an additional avenue for corporations to stop Canadian governments from implementing new programs or from reversing the privatization decisions of previous governments.

Competition Policy, Monopolies And State Enterprises

A fourth major chapter which will have a profound impact on public programs and public enterprises in Canada is Chapter Fifteen. This chapter, in particular, reveals the strong anti-public sector bias of the free trade deal.

Chapter Fifteen is a chapter not included in the FTA. The earlier agreement had several short sections under a single article (Article 2010: Monopolies) which was included in the second-last chapter of the FTA, under the general heading "Chapter Twenty: Other Provisions". However, the new NAFTA chapter constitutes nothing less than a frontal assault on Canada's public enterprises, agencies and Crown corporations.

The first article in the chapter (Article 1501: Competition Law) contains three short paragraphs, the first two setting out homilies about the benefits of competition and the need to deter firms from anti-competitive practices. Incredibly, the third says that the trade agreement does not apply to these practices. In other words, it is not intended to regulate international cartels, market carve-ups by multinational companies and a variety of other anti-competitive practices engaged in at the international level by global corporations. (So much for the commitment to free markets.)

The second article imposes new restrictions on what are described as "monopolies and state enterprises." It requires that before a government can set up a new public enterprise, it must consult with the other parties of NAFTA. In setting up these new public entities, it must comply with the nullification and impairment sections of Annex 2004, which are designed to ensure that private firms do not suffer as a result of new public programs or enterprises being established.

Subsection 3 of Article 1502 contains a wide range of new rules which are intended to ensure that all current and future government enterprises operate according to commercial principles.

The point of these detailed rules is clear: to ensure that, in future, public enterprises can only operate on the basis of commercial considerations. All other public policy objectives are to be abandoned.

Chapter Fifteen applies to federal and provincial Crown corporations and agencies as well as certain publicly-regulated private companies which have been given monopoly rights to provide a good or service by the federal government or a province.[11]

What Chapter Fifteen reveals, more than any other chapter, is the explicitly commercial philosophy underlying NAFTA.

Not only is the deal structured to push as many public activities as possible into the private sector: it is designed to 'commercialize' the mandate of those which do remain in the public sector.

Intellectual Property Rights

An area of NAFTA that deserves a good deal more public scrutiny, particularly by the educational community, is the new chapter on intellectual property rights, Chapter Seventeen. The incorporation of a wide range of new provisions governing patents, trademarks, sound recordings, satellite signals, semiconductor designs, trade secrets, computer software, biotechnology and a range of other matters lumped together under the umbrella heading of "intellectual property rights" has been a longstanding objective of U.S. policy. This component of NAFTA was not part of the FTA, and constitutes a major expansion of the deal.

The concept of intellectual property has been extensively promoted during the past decade by the large multinational firms who want to obtain legal protection for their patents. They have waged an energetic campaign against Third-World countries who have borrowed their discoveries without paying them royalties. They have vigorously lobbied GATT and other international organizations for international rules with teeth which would enable them to force countries with lax enforcement standards to crack down on the unauthorized use of their 'intellectual property'.

Chapter Seventeen of NAFTA contains 29 detailed pages setting out the scope of the obligations entered into by Canada, the types of intellectual property to be protected, the protection mechanisms and the enforcement provisions. The chapter incorporates the principle of national treatment for individuals and firms who wish to register their patent in the countries covered by the deal. National treatment includes the rights of, for example, U.S. companies or citizens to require the Canadian government to enforce their patent rights as if they were Canadian patent holders.

Certain sections of Chapter Seventeen require Canada to introduce new criminal laws. For example, under Article 1717:

Criminal Procedures and Penalties, Canada takes on the following obligations:

1. Each Party shall provide criminal procedures and penalties to be applied at least in cases of wilful trademark counterfeiting or copyright piracy on a commercial scale. Each Party shall provide that penalties available include imprisonment or monetary fines, or both, sufficient to provide a deterrent, consistent with the level of penalties applied for crimes of a corresponding gravity.
2. Each party shall provide that, in appropriate cases, its judicial authorities may order the seizure, forfeiture and destruction of infringing goods and of any materials and implements the predominant use of which has been in the commission of the offence.

The chapter on intellectual property rights has very profound implications for education in a wide range of areas.

It applies to the new technology which increasingly will be playing a role in education at all levels, including a range of interactive computer and audio-visual learning devices. It covers out-of-country cable and satellite transmission of proprietary educational programs, courses and learning aids which have been given copyright of patent protection.

The intellectual property rights section will provide a plethora of new ways in which corporations can extract royalties from our public educational system. In this respect, it will have major, but as yet uncalculated, financial implications for fiscally hardpressed schools and universities. An analogy with what is happening to our health-care system as a result of the granting of new intellectual property rights to the multinational drug firms may illustrate some of these concerns.

The negative impact on Canada's health-care system and Canadian consumers of the free-trade-related commitment to extend brand-name pharmaceutical patent protection for up to 20 years has already been the subject of major public concern. The first part of this process came with the enactment in 1987 of Bill C-22 which extended patent monopolies from 7 to 10 years. It is estimated that this decision raised drug costs by an average of 16 per cent. The federal government denied that there was any connection between this legislation and the FTA, but subsequent events have exposed this fiction.

In anticipation of NAFTA's implementation, the federal government has already enacted Bill C-91 which extends patent protection for brand-name pharmaceuticals to 20 years. The provisions of the bill parallel the new 'rights' given to the drug firms under NAFTA. This time the federal government acknowledged that the legislation was related to free trade. The costs to Canadians have been variously estimated as up to $800 million annually by the time the full impact of the new legislation is felt.

The private drug companies benefitting from this change are almost entirely foreign-controlled. Consequently, most of this money will leave the country. It will have the negative effect of exporting jobs, draining our balance of payments, and pushing up costs to provincial government drug plans. This latter consequence will sharply increase pressure to reduce the scope and coverage of pharmaceutical-care programs for seniors, welfare recipients and others requiring extensive drug therapy.

While the drug patent issue has received the most attention, many other aspects of the new chapter on intellectual property rights will profoundly affect Canadians and particularly the educational community. At its core, this chapter involves a commitment to the 'privatization' and 'commercialization' of knowledge. It treats knowledge as a commodity which is the property of those who first get their lawyers to the patent office. And, once given patent protection, its enables those who 'own' it — and we are talking here almost exclusively about large multinational companies — to extract financial benefit for allowing others the privilege of using it.

The granting of so-called intellectual property rights to the multinational firms which control production and distribution of drugs, computer software, biotechnology, entertainment, agricultural products and the like is the equivalent in the 1990s of the 18th-century enclosure movement which stole the common land from the peasantry in England and redistributed it to those members of the nobility and gentry sufficiently influential to have Acts of Enclosure passed by Parliament in their interest. The behaviour of the multinational firms mirrors precisely this history of privatization of common property.

Enshrining intellectual property rights in NAFTA entails a commitment to transfer much of the common heritage of Canadians and, indeed, of all peoples to the private control of profit-driven corporations.[12] It is, in part, the looting of our common cultural and intellectual heritage. It will stifle the transmission of ideas and knowledge, while placing new restrictions on the free flow of ideas within Canada and throughout the hemisphere.

The obsession with creating private property out of knowledge will profoundly influence the free flow of ideas, information and knowledge, particularly in the university sector. More of our publicly-funded research will end up monopolized by private firms with links to individual universities — links which give them the right to patent new discoveries for commercial benefit.

Major new costs will also be imposed on our educational institutions in a manner paralleling the cost increases in the brand-name drug sector. Hardpressed universities and other educational institutions will have to find new money to reimburse private multinational firms for the right to make use of an increasing array of copyrighted research materials and patented processes and substances. New staff will be required to calculate the royalties owing, 'enforce' patents and educate students and faculty about their new obligations. There will also be new concerns about protecting 'trade secrets' — concerns which will act to stifle the publication of research which could have commercial applications.

The authors are unaware of any federal government study which attempts to assess the effects, financial or operational, of these new rules on our education system. Yet there is no question that, in the very near future, educators at all levels will be confronted with the task of ensuring that Canadian educational practices conform to the prerogatives given multinational corporations over their intellectual property rights.

Telecommunications For Private Interests

NAFTA includes an entirely new chapter on telecommunications. It sets up an international framework to protect the private investments of telecommunications firms, while opening up publicly-owned-and-operated systems to private interests. Telecommunications is treated simply as a profit-making industry which should be largely freed of any government regulation or interference. In the process, all other approaches to telecommunications are displaced. The fact that a communications system is the vehicle through which a nation speaks to itself, or that a telecommunications system has cultural and other non-economic functions, is simply ignored.

In terms of Canada's legislation, the *Broadcasting Act* has been used to regulate the media, including radio, television and cable, while the soon-to-be-replaced *Railway Act*, the *Radio-communication Act* and the *Department of Communications Act* apply to telegraph, telephone and other electronic data transmission systems.[13] However, the distinctions between these areas are increasingly blurred. Traditional regulatory mechanisms are being overtaken by new technology which makes existing rules obsolete or unenforceable. This calls for a re-examination of how we regulate our electronic airways. However, the presumption in NAFTA is that we should move towards deregulating our telecommunications system so that commercial considerations can be given full sway.

The implications are significant for education. To the extent that the remaining domestic components of our radio, television and cable systems fall under the control of large multinational telecommunications corporations, it will be increasingly difficult — and increasingly costly — for domestic public educational institutions to produce Canadian educational programs or to gain access to the system for the promotion of educational objectives in Canada.

The new chapter on telecommunications will also affect cultural practices. Canada's culture is deeply intertwined with the means of communicating it. Without the ability to transmit information, ideas and cultural endeavours, Canadians are restricted in their ability to participate in the evolution of their common culture.

There is another dimension to this issue. Giant U.S. media corporations such as Whittle Communications are expanding into the area of 'educational television'. In the U.S. they are offering underfunded public schools the opportunity of acquiring badly needed technology in return for allowing them to show their educational programs in the classroom. The catch is that the programs contain commercials targeted at the captive student audience. Whittle now operates in over 10,000 schools and reaps about $630,000 per day from school-directed commercials.

A Canadian equivalent of the highly commercial Channel One which has expanded rapidly into U.S. classrooms has emerged: Youth News Network (YNN). This 'educational television' firm has approached school boards in a number of provinces including Quebec, Ontario and Nova Scotia. The pitch is to offer 12 minutes of television, including two minutes of commercials.[15] In return, school boards will receive TVs, videos, a satellite dish and other related audio-visual equipment. Its establishment in Canada is further described in Chapter Five.

In addition to the concerns about YNN raised by parents, teachers and others in the educational community, there is another issue related to the concept of national treatment under NAFTA. YNN is currently viewed as a Canadian operation. But it could easily be bought out by a U.S. media corporation intent on showing U.S.-produced material which it is already producing. Those who think this far-fetched need only turn on their local cable-TV station to see what happens when broadcasting regulations protecting Canadian culture are relaxed.

Another area of telecommunications policy which will be affected by NAFTA is the cross-border provision of 'educational services'. Already, in anticipation of NAFTA, we are witnessing a veritable deluge of advertising on cable television networks by U.S.-based educational corporations. These companies offer a wide variety of commercial, for-profit educational services. Some offer diplomas and degrees by correspondence in accounting, business management, trades, secretarial, office and computer work. Others offer educational services such as cooking, exercise programs, D.I.Y. kits and the like which border on the 'recreational' side of the learning process.

These developments are encouraging both the 'privatization' and the 'Americanization' of education. The exemption of U.S. and Mexican firms from having to have a 'local presence' means that these corporations can offer their services by 1-800 numbers without being required even to have an office in Canada.

This constitutes a major erosion of the constitutional rights of provincial governments who, ostensibly, have the authority to regulate both public and private educational services. Despite the absence of provincial consent, NAFTA grants new 'rights' to telecommunications firms who are already broadcasting educational programming or educational advertisements directly into Canadian homes.

The decisions by a Tory-appointed CRTC in anticipation of the new arrangements under NAFTA have already permitted a dramatic expansion in the cross-border sale of private educational services. The CRTC is systematically deregulating the airways, permitting greater penetration of the Canadian market by U.S. firms. NAFTA will lock these changes into place, making it virtually impossible for provincial governments to exercise their constitutional right to regulate educational service providers.

In short, there is enormous scope for the private media and educational service companies to expand their control of the telecommunications systems evolving in Canada. NAFTA provides a framework for them to do so.

Greater Than The Sum Of Its Parts

As it should by now be obvious, the NAFTA deal is a complex legal document which imposes a wide range of new 'rules' on government while granting a wide range of new 'rights' to multinational corporations. Its chapters and provisions are deeply interconnected, with concepts such as 'national treatment' woven throughout the fabric of the agreement.

But it is important not simply to focus on specific provisions, significant as they may be for particular aspects of our educational system. For in the case of NAFTA, the whole is greater than the sum of its parts. NAFTA constitutes the legal framework of a commitment to unleash hemispheric market forces throughout our economy and society. The legal framework is designed to reinforce the power of corporations to privatize and commercialize our economy, while blocking the ability of democratically elected governments to regulate their profit-driven activities.

Chapter Three

Free Trade and the U.S. Model of Education

Free trade will likely have little impact on education in the United States. Neither NAFTA nor the Canada-U.S. agreement before it will shift education in the U.S. from the issues and directions defined by history and ideology and produced by current economic and social pressures in that country. That is because no equal exchange in education policies will take place among the North American countries. Rather, harmonization will be a one-way process, with the ideology, issues and structures of the dominant country — the United States — significantly imposed in Canada and Mexico.

The formal mechanisms of the trade agreement will assist in this harmonization to a U.S. model. They will also take further, and solidify, changes that are already happening. The education system in Mexico has already been partially reshaped by the Mexican government increasingly to resemble the system in the United States. Similar pressures exist in Canada, with the agenda being set by corporate pressure groups like the Corporate-Higher Education Forum and the Business Council on National Issues (BCNI), by the federal government with its "Prosperity Initiative", and by the business press with calls for national goals and national testing.

Although factors other than free trade are reshaping U.S. education, an understanding of trends in the American education system will give sharper focus to the nature of the reforms being urged on Canada and Mexico by the ideology and interests that are also behind the free trade agreements.

The Common School

American public schools have their roots in the 19th-century "Common School Crusade". The crusaders included some of those who saw the public school as a central institution in producing and maintaining a democratic society. However, many other groups saw other uses for public schools.

The mid-19th century was a period of social upheaval, industrialization, large-scale immigration and urbanization. A common belief that education could help to bring stability out of the chaos was translated into the creation of the public school. For differing reasons, a wide range of groups across political, regional and class lines created a consensus about public education.

The consensus, according to a description in a recent Washington Education Association publication, included the following elements:

1) The common school was to be public, not private. It was to be free — paid for by general taxpayers, not tuition and fees. It was not a pauper system, but a public system — so fine as to be a place where the wealthiest would send their children.

2) The schools would be managed by lay boards.

3) Schools would teach the 3 R's but would also promote individual and civic virtue to preserve morality and the republic. Values would be instilled to shape character and to create a productive work force — values of family, religion, work and thrift. Uniform textbooks — mainly the early McGuffey Readers — were the first powerful institutional tool to instill these values.

4) Industrialists and taxpayers, since they were footing the bill, wanted the schools to be cost efficient. Horace Mann and his colleagues turned to the education system in Prussia for direct instructional techniques — classrooms of 40 to 60 stu-

dents with bolted down chairs and standard textbooks so the same lesson could be delivered by the teacher in the same way to the entire group. They grouped children into grades by age for bureaucratic efficiency and simplicity. A uniform course of study was later initiated and an examination system was put in place, first at the elementary and later at the secondary level.

5) Finally, the last major part of the common school vision of the 1800's was the screening mechanism applied to students. From the economic viewpoint of the day, about 20 per cent were needed to be the leaders — factory owners, doctors, lawyers, etc. They needed to learn to lead, to think, to set goals and to run institutions. Another 30 per cent needed a strong enough education to carry out the dictates of the leaders in an effective and efficient manner — professionals, white collar workers, mid-management. In the bottom half of the student group, about 30 per cent could be functionally illiterate as long as they had the correct values about work, obedience, family obligation, and could carry out the mindless, repetitive tasks of the factory. Thinking, in those industrial age work environments was not only unnecessary, but problematic. Memorizing and conditioned responding were a more "appropriate" preparation for an authoritarian work system. The last 20 per cent were not needed in the industrial work place of the 1800's and were generally thought to be incapable of learning anyway. They were the throw-aways.

The Darwinian survival-of-the-fittest view of the world, with its neatly drawn bell-shaped curves, reinforced by Calvinist pessimism about human nature, seemed to match perfectly the economic needs of the industrialists. This is the powerful combination of ideas that produced the screening mechanism still undergirding, and now undermining, the structure of schools. By the early 1900s, the bell curve was taken from Darwin's work and applied to groups of learners as a description of the distribution of their intellectual abilities.[1]

This short but comprehensive description of the nature of the common school gives an idea of how integrally the public schools have both shaped and been shaped by the economic and social systems in the United States.

This system has several defining elements that are key. It is important to identify these — and the changes that have taken place in these elements in the last 15 years — to see clearly the pressures that are and will be put on Canadian public schools to harmonize them with American education.

The Myth Of Equality

First is the myth of a society without social classes and with equality of opportunity. The fact that the schools were free from tuition charges, and that the wealthy and powerful sent their own children to the public school, helped to feed this myth. However, as the description of the common school makes clear, within the school systems of testing, sorting and tracking largely reproduced the existing class and power relationships. Opportunities opened by economic expansion allowed enough people from immigrant or working-class backgrounds to move up the economic and social ladders to reinforce the myth of a completely open system.

Second, the common school was the agency of the "melting pot", the process of taking diverse (but primarily white, European) immigrant groups, stripping away their old-country identity, and incorporating them into the identity of being American.

A major group, of course, was largely excluded from this process — people of African heritage, especially in the South. If they were not excluded entirely from schooling, they attended schools that were 'separate, but equal', a category that was accepted in the law until the Brown vs. Board of Education Supreme Court decision in 1954. In fact, the inferior black schools were "the result of conscious plans by industrial leaders to segregate the Black population and educate them as an inexpensive labour force for the new industrial South."[2]

Third, the common school served as an important agency of what Noam Chomsky calls "the manufacturing of consent." The domination of the social consensus reflected in these schools leaves many Americans without the intellectual tools ('crap detectors', as they were called in the '60s) to identify social and political issues as choices that could go beyond those of the two dominant political parties. The spirit of this approach was captured by a high-school teacher who in 1921 said that the school prepared the student for a society that demanded "a sort of social like-mindedness."[3]

Finally, workers had to be prepared to serve industry, and business leaders played an influential role in deciding that this happen at school. The apparent contradiction between egalitarian premises and the need for differentiated preparation for differentiated roles in the economy was resolved through testing and tracking, making it appear as if ability, not background, determined success.

The reality, however, has been "that the schools throughout the history of American education have been used as instruments to teach the norms necessary to adjust the young to the changing patterns of the economic system as well as to the society's more permanent values."[4]

Twentieth-Century Innovations

Political progressivism and the emerging domination of the large corporation in the economy brought with them two innovations.

John Dewey is the person most associated with progressivism as applied to education. "From Dewey's point of view knowledge was a product of social conditions. The learning process, Dewey felt, should be a part of an active solution to a social problem."[5]

The progressive education movement "argued that schools should be free to focus on the ultimate objectives of public education: the development of the critical learning and thinking skills; and the attitudes, values, and interests necessary for effective growth, development, and functioning as members of a free and democratic society."[6]

While Dewey and the other progressives may have had a significant influence on what many who taught in the schools thought they were doing, the progressives' radical democratic ideals were largely not adopted in practice. "Dewey had wanted to replace the mechanical atmosphere in the classroom with social activity so that social unity would be the result of social understanding."[7] Neither progressive pedagogy nor federal court-ordered desegregation produced the conditions for the egalitarian democracy they aimed to achieve.

Another very significant feature added to the schools in the early 20th century was the domination by a bureaucratic hierarchy of professional administrators. The early schools were characterized by a close tie with the community through small districts with elected school boards. As American industry increasingly became centralized into large corporations, school governance also changed. Amalgamation into larger school districts was accompanied by the development of management forms that were similar to those of corporations. Communication and control travelled from the chief officer through a hierarchy of other levels of management and, finally, to teacher and students.

Is this, then, the kind of school system that Canada can expect to find its schools measured against in a 'harmonized' North America? Not necessarily. Economic and social changes have brought the American school system into new areas of contention. Some of these areas are already familiar in Canadian eduction as well.

Recent Challenges To U.S. Schools

Two powerful economic and social changes are having to be taken into account by the school system in the United States. One is the changing nature of the economy; the other is the changing makeup of the population.

The central function of the school system — preparing the young for the economic system — has not diminished. In fact, it has taken on new urgency. Patricia Graham, professor of history of education at Harvard University, says:

> The disappearance of jobs for the unskilled in America, either because companies found it cheaper to have those tasks done abroad where wages were lower or because new manufacturing processes still left in the United States required higher skill levels, precipitated the current public concern about the quality of the American schools and the academic insufficiency of many new entrants to the work force.[8]

At the same time, those least well served by the melting-pot definition of America and its schools — people of colour — are dramatically increasing in numbers. Forty per cent of school children in the year 2000 will be children of colour; the majority in most urban school districts already are.[9]

The political expression of alarm at these facts was expressed in the report "A Nation at Risk", prepared for the U.S. Secretary of Education early in Ronald Reagan's first term as president. While the report accepted the ideal of the common school with democratic social goals, the view of education as an economic function and a chauvinist sense of national destiny come through clearly in the opening paragraphs of the report:

> Our Nation is at risk. Our once unchallenged preeminence in commerce, industry, science, and technological innovation is being overtaken by competitors throughout the world. This report is concerned with only one of the many causes and dimensions of the problem, but it is the one that undergirds American prosperity, security and civility. We report to the American people that while we can take justifiable pride in what our schools and colleges have historically accomplished and contributed to the United States and the well-being of its people, the educational foundations of our society are presently being eroded by a rising tide of mediocrity that threatens our very future as a Nation and a people. What was unimaginable a generation ago has begun to occur — others are matching and surpassing our educational attainments.
>
> If an unfriendly foreign power had attempted to impose on America the mediocre educational performance that exists today, we might well have viewed it as an act of war. As it stands, we have allowed this to happen to ourselves.... We have, in effect, been committing an act of unthinking, unilateral educational disarmament.[10]

The Right's Agenda

What did the commission say should be done about this? Keep more kids in school — create "high retention rates in schools and colleges." Define new expectations in "hard work, behaviour, self-discipline, and motivation." Offer fewer electives and more math and science and computer science. Make the school year longer. Set national goals and check with standardized tests to see that the goals are being met.

In the article "Restructuring Students for Restructured Work", Ray and Mickelson say that "A Nation at Risk" confirmed 'cocktail party fears' and tapped into pent-up business concerns.[11] They go on to examine two of the chief themes of business demands on schools: the 'competitiveness' problem and demands of the high-tech society.

"The blame," they say, "for U.S. capitalists' weakness in world markets is placed increasingly on working-class and low-income students" — the dropouts. One business task force they worked with "attributed the rise in poverty to individual behaviours and life-styles: teenage mothers, single-parent families, illiteracy, and drug abuse.... Not one member linked the increasing rates of poverty or the lack of motivation ... with the kinds of jobs that companies have eliminated and created over the past several years."[12]

Another widely repeated claim is that schools must produce better educated workers to match the rapidly growing number of new high-tech jobs. "The theme," Ray and Mickelson say, "implies the widespread availability and expansion of sophisticated, complex jobs requiring a solid academic background."[13]

These demands for high-tech workers are greatly exaggerated. There is evidence that "the economy is generating nine new cashiering jobs for every computer programming job."[14] The U.S. Bureau of Labor Statistics has reported "that although 23.4 to 28.6 million new jobs will have been created between 1982 and 1995, only 1 million to 4.6 million will be in high-tech industries."[15]

Despite the discrepancy between rhetoric and reality, "A Nation at Risk" was followed during the Reagan years by a series of reports reiterating the need for high-tech preparation through the schools. State legislatures in all 50 states mandated reforms which have, in effect, "resulted in some state legislatures becoming super school boards that have mandated strict rules for teachers and students."[15] These reforms adopted the ideological perspectives and the language of corporate boardrooms.

How Business Defines The Agenda

The American public school system is very decentralized, with elected school boards having the direct authority over the schools, subject to the rules set by state legislatures and the requirements to qualify for federal funding for targeted programs. Curriculum decisions are often made at the school level, not even at the district or state level. Yet business influence is exercised in a number of ways. The overall ideological climate has been set by panels and reports, both at the national and state levels. Some of these are directly commissioned by government, such as "A Nation at Risk". Others are produced by foundations that were created by corporate money such as the Carnegie and Ford foundations. Business representatives nearly always play a key role in these specially-commissioned panels.

Corporate influence is also exercised by groups that bring business leaders together to define their common interests. The corporate agenda for education is not some secret conspiracy. It has been openly described in publications by organizations that have names and addresses. In the U.S., one of the most significant of these organizations is the Business Roundtable. It lists addresses — 200 Park Avenue in New York and 1615 L Street, N.W. in Washington — that are at the heart of corporate and government power centres.[16]

Created in 1972, the Business Roundtable is made up of the chief executives of 200 of the major corporations with headquarters in the United States. The purpose of the organization is to develop a consensus among the corporate leaders on policy issues and then to advocate those positions. The central purpose of the group is "less unwarranted intrusion by government into business affairs."[17]

The Roundtable's Ad Hoc Committee on Education of senior executives was set up in 1978 because of the critical importance of education to the productivity and competitiveness of business. In 1988 it published "The Role of Business in Education Reform: Blueprint for Action". The Roundtable was concerned that if education paid for by the public was not adequate in providing skills for work, then the cost to corporations for training "could increase dramatically and become an insurmountable obstacle to U.S. international competitiveness." David Noble describes this motivation as socializing the cost and privatizing the benefits.

The Ad Hoc committee identified strategies for business. One recommendation was to provide a sustained commitment to a limited number of programs. Math, science and reading comprehension were singled out because "when American students score at the top in math, science, and reading comprehension, American business will gain in the global marketplace."[19] A second call was for national minimum curriculum standards. The Ad Hoc committee said teachers should be rewarded not through smaller classes or better teaching conditions, but through incentives as they are understood in business — merit pay, rewards and recognition for superior performance.

Business Controls School Boards

Business operates in education not just in the policy and lobbying arena. School boards are also largely controlled by people from business. Studies have shown that "most boards of education in the U.S. have generally been composed disproportionably of white, male business owners and professionals."[20]

Business influence extends, as well, to the school level. The Business Roundtable is by no means alone in promoting school/business partnerships. A regular feature of education workshops and conferences is the promotion of these partnerships. Most American communities have some form of project to build cooperation between educators and business leaders.[21]

Teachers and administrators often resort to these partnerships out of desperation because of lack of adequate resources. Reduced taxation saves megabucks for business. To give this some context, $156 million is less than what corporations save in a single year from tax breaks in a single medium-sized state, Wisconsin. Yet $156 million was the total spent by all corporations nationally on public schools combined over several years in the late 1980s.[22]

The small amount they donate can produce significant influence for business. The money contributed becomes a business expense for tax purposes, offering a financial rebate to the company. Perhaps most importantly, the business gets public relations gains from these donations by appearing to be responsible. Charity from business, rather than taxation of business, puts power in the hands of business to set the agenda for education.

An "Education President" Wants Privatization

George Bush characterized himself as the "Education President". He should have called himself the education-privatizing president.

Early in Bush's term, he announced six national education goals under the title of America 2000: all children will start school ready to learn, 90 per cent of high school students will graduate, students will be competent in basic subjects, U.S. students will be first in mathematics and science, every American adult will be literate and possess the skills necessary to compete in a global economy, and schools will be drug-free and safe.

These goals provide an insight into the social problems of the U.S. as much as they define the purpose of schooling in terms of economic competition.

Even more telling are the key strategies Bush proposed for making changes in American schools. He wanted to set goals nationally and use tests and "indicators" to see if the goals were being met. Yet while setting goals centrally, he wanted "accountability" for meeting them to be local, not national. Also, he wanted to increase the role of the private sector in education.

The political push for these directions is not likely to disappear with Bush's evacuation of the White House. The Democratic Leadership Council, of which Bill Clinton was a prominent member, virtually rubber-stamped the initiative when it was announced.[23]

On the surface, it may appear that there is a contradiction between the centralization of goal-setting to the national level, while at the same time decentralizing responsibility and accountability right down to the school level with various school-based, decision-making schemes. In fact, however, this model reflects the changes in the structures of management developed by the transnational corporations in the globalized economy. During most of this century, major corporations operated with a bureaucratic structure, with directions on goals and how they were to be achieved moving down a hierarchical line from the centre, and information moving up the same line from the place of production or sales, so that further decisions could be made centrally and passed down. The bureaucratic structure of school systems also followed this pattern.

Information technology has dramatically changed the process of management. The global corporation still has a group at the centre, still setting goals. How those goals are to be achieved, however, is less likely to be set at the central level and passed down. Rather, responsibility rests with those running a particular unit of the company to make decisions that, while in keeping with the company's overall goals, are achieved by fitting with the local situation. Local managers are to be held accountable for results, not for following regulations.

As illustrations, IBM and Apple are two global corporations that have recently broken apart their traditional structures to set up separate, smaller groupings to compete in particular areas, with the managers being given responsibility for determining how best to operate and made directly accountable for the results. These new structures are supposed to be more flexible and thus able to be more competitive in rapidly changing situations.

As many have pointed out, middle management positions have disappeared during the past decade and the middle class is in decline. The crucial communication role that middle managers played in the corporation is being replaced by technology. Information and feedback can go directly from the centre to the place of production or sales and back, without the necessity of the layers of command that, in the past, played a crucial role in communications.

How Business Gets Feedback

These organizational models drawn from business are now being pressed on the education system. The new role of the central state is to set overall goals and to run a feedback or indicator system that tells how well the goals are being met. The feedback system in America 2000 is primarily a set of national tests. They play the role that profit information would play in the corporate system. Thus, direction can take place and be monitored without the formal hierarchical administrative line that once was essential to attempt to direct a large system. The goals and monitoring system for America 2000 reflects this application from the methods of operation of the global, transnational corporation to the reform of the schools.

Stanford University's Larry Cuban says truth-in-advertising should require that this grafting of business methods onto education be called what it is: "an experiment on children that has no scientific basis."[24] The basic assumption underlying a report card on school results is that test scores reflect the academic quality of the schools. In reality, they will be more accurate as a general index of the educational, economic, and social advantages of class, because they don't account for opportunities lost to poverty, racial and cultural discrimination.[25]

What's Meant By 'Choice'

The other key adaptation from the corporate world in America 2000 is the emphasis on 'choice'. This is the latest version of the application of the free-market ideology, proposed for education three decades ago by the dean of right-wing economists, Milton Friedman.

The purpose of 'choice' is made clear in an article in the *Kappan* by Denis Doyle from the Hudson Institute, one of the American right-wing think tanks. Doyle says:

> ... choice means an environment in which individual consumers — clients — would actually be free to abandon schools that are failing, an environment in which teachers and principals could escape from the tender mercies of senior administrators and school boards. The one thing a monopolist fears above all other things is choice; it is the enemy of apparatchiks everywhere, the enemy of central planners.[26]

However, an important part of the choice agenda is revealed by the fact that "the first choice program provided white students in Virginia public funds to attend private academies in order to avoid attending public schools with Blacks."[27]

The 'choice' agenda has sufficient momentum that 37 states to have considered 'choice' legislation in 1992, according to the Center for Choice in Education, a part of the U.S. Department of Education.

Proposals for 'vouchers' that would allow parents to get taxpayer support to send their children to private schools — another form of 'choice' — have been around for decades. California is holding a referendum in November, 1993 on whether to adopt a voucher system. California's education system has more students than in all of Canada, and could be an influential foot in the door for vouchers.[28]

The California proposal is being sold by proponents as a money-saving device. Such savings are based on an assumption that the private sector would create a massive expansion of low-cost private schools. The objective is for private schools to capture 40 per cent of student enrolment within a decade, up from the current 10 per cent. In this regard, Jonathan Kozol quotes a *New York Times* report that a "growing bunch of entrepreneurs are suggesting that unabashed capitalism can succeed" in the delivery of education "where bureaucracy and altruism have failed."

So you have the Burger King firm opening fully-accredited, quasi-private high schools — "Burger King Academies". And at a Boulder, Colorado high school, "McDonald's supplies not only the food but the curriculum: Pupils study McDonald's inventory, payroll and ordering procedures in math; McDonald's menu plans in home economics; and the company's marketing practices in business class."[29]

Campbell's Soup offers a deal as well: the film strip "Boyhood of Abraham Lincoln" for 5,125 labels; a remote control projector to show it for 20,000 more labels; and a screen for 6,750. That can be followed by Chef Boyardee lesson materials on nutrition.[30]

Corporations are also heavily into providing propaganda for the classroom. According to a study by Ralph Nader's organization, free curriculum materials are provided schools by nearly two-thirds of the largest U.S. corporations.[31]

Probably the best-known education entrepreneur is Chris Whittle, who runs Channel One, the news and ads TV program shown in 10,000 schools across the United States. The program is required viewing for eight million students daily — more than a third of all teenagers in the United States. When schools sign up for Channel One, they make a commitment to have at least 90 per cent of their students watch its program every day.

The large number of viewers enables Whittle to charge very profitable ad rates. At $120,000 per 30 seconds, it brings in at least twice as much as on a top-rated network news program.[32] One study of the impact of Channel One on students indicates that they don't gain any more knowledge about the news, but they do have a higher view of advertised products than do students who don't view it. The fact that the ads are shown in school gives an implicit endorsation to the products.

Whittle also heads Project Edison, a plan to create a chain of profit-making private schools across the United States. A major shareholder is Time Warner, the media conglomerate that has huge holdings in a range of film, publication and other media outlets. Whittle expects funding as well from Walt Disney Co. and PepsiCo, Inc. Whittle's plan is to turn a profit by saving on teacher salaries by using volunteers, classroom aids and computers for instruction.

A company called Education Alternatives Inc. (EAI) has contracts with public school boards to run schools in a number of school districts throughout the United States. The company operates as a corporation selling stocks; it raised more than $40 million in three public stock offerings.

EAI offers a teaching philosophy as part of its package including co-operative learning, whole language, intensive use of computers and other activity-centred forms of education. It has packaged the approach and registered it under a company trademark, and has done the same with Personal Education Plans, a package for setting individualized student goals. A core element of EAI's approach is "continuous, computer-controlled monitoring of student and teacher performance."[33]

One district that had a contract with EAI discovered some of the complexity of the relationship: "When you hire an outside company to come in and run your school system and they supply the superintendent, who does that superintendent work for? The company or the school board?"[34]

Kozol, author of *Savage Inequalities,* identified three fundamental concerns about the growing direct domination of the schools by business.

"First," he said, "if these ventures are not profitable, the demands of any corporation will require that they either cut back services, screen out the difficult students or simply shut down." Second, he said, is a fear that business ideology will creep into the schools. Third, even if a business-operated school leaves the curriculum intact, certain characteristics of American business "are conveyed completely apart from curriculum or textbooks — for example, just the idea that competition is the best way to generate success, which relies upon an unwarranted faith in the virtues of unmitigated individualism."[35]

Clearly, the first principle of the American common school — that it was to be public, not private, and was to be free, without tuition — has been abandoned by powerful forces in American society.

Patterns in American education have long followed the shaping and reshaping taking place in the economy. Services that were once an unquestioned part of the public sector are facing pressures to move them into the marketplace. One of the central elements of the FTA, and even more so of NAFTA, is the idea of opening services — not just goods — to the realm and rules of the marketplace and trade.

It is difficult to place much credence in the assurances given by former International Trade Minister Michael Wilson that education is protected from being affected by NAFTA. If the marketplace push in American education gains complete dominance, the national border and the different traditions of Canada will provide little protection against the export of ideology and institutions from the U.S. to a country 'harmonized' nearly out of existence.

Chapter Four

NAFTA And Education In Mexico

"... [T]he expansion of foreign investment in Mexico, and in other countries of Latin America, is likely to have important long-term impacts on the education systems in those countries and perhaps that of the United States. This conclusion is based on experiences in the economic integration of Europe and the already-observed effects of expanded transnational investment in Latin America. The long-term effect will be to reduce diversity between national educational systems in the direction of greater emphasis on technical and applied knowledge and skills." — Noel F. McGinn[1]

To obtain a broader perspective on the corporate forces shaping the direction of educational change in Canada under free trade, it is helpful to examine recent developments in Mexico. A review of the changes implemented since 1982, and particularly since the government of Carlos Salinas de Gortari opted to negotiate a free trade agreement with Canada and the U.S., reveals many disturbing parallels with Canadian trends.

Indeed, the parallels are uncanny. Corporations in Mexico are making demands identical to those of business in Canada. They want the educational curriculum at all levels to focus on practical, economic objectives designed to make Mexico more 'competitive' in the global economy. They wish to see Mexico's public school system adopt a much more commercial orientation, so that firms operating in Mexico will have access to workers with the skills, training and work habits required by multinational business as part of a new international division of labour. Simultaneously, the corporations want Mexico to abandon its populist cultural, historical and regional curriculum — a curriculum based on the progressive, egalitarian traditions of the Mexican Revolution.

Business also has a parallel agenda for education finance in Mexico. With the support of the International Monetary Fund (IMF) and the World Bank, corporations have encouraged the federal government to reduce public spending by 'off-loading' much of its budgetary responsibility for education to state and local levels.

At the same time, business has called for a tightening of the federal government's central control over curriculum. Thus responsibility for providing educational resources will fall increasingly on hardpressed state governments, while control over the content of education will remain centralized in the federal education ministry.

There has been a strong push to privatize parts of the public educational system in Mexico, especially in the areas of post-secondary education and skills training. There has also been a growing demand to 'commercialize' the focus of the curriculum in the primary and secondary schools. And there has been a major effort to give business interests greater access to the governance of educational institutions, while reducing the historic role of other groups in the educational community such as teachers, students, unions and local communities. New opportunities are also being created for the expansion of private educational institutions.

At the university level, the same pattern of growing corporate involvement through 'seed' money and 'partnerships' with universities which has emerged in Canada is also apparent in Mexico. Business has also succeeded in getting the government to use its financial clout to change university priorities. Subsidies, grants and research monies are being targeted at disciplines which are believed to have commercial value, while being denied to other, more traditional, academic disciplines. The focus of the university system is being consciously shifted from liberal arts to science, engineering and business administration.

In sum, Mexico is witnessing the transformation of its entire educational system to accommodate the labour market requirements of multinational corporations and their domestic cheerleaders. The NAFTA is now the cornerstone of this process, for it is designed to lock in, permanently, the economic, social and educational changes carried out by the Salinas government.

However, Mexico has gone further than Canada in one area. The government has carried out a major rewriting of the recent history of the country — as presented in the new national curriculum pushed through by the Salinas government — to wipe out the nationalist heritage of the revolution of 1910. The achievements of the revolution, particularly in areas such as literacy and popular education, have been largely written out of the new textbooks.

To understand what has been occurring in the Mexican educational system in the past decade, it is necessary first to examine the structure of the system and its recent history.

Overview Of Education In Mexico

For Canadians, the first thing of note about Mexican education is its size. There are almost as many students in the Mexican educational system as there are people in Canada. According to Ministry of Education (SEP) figures, in the 1990-91 academic year 25,086,800 students were enrolled at all levels in Mexican educational institutions.[2] Of these, 14,401,600 students were enrolled in primary schools; 4,190,200 in junior secondary schools; 1,721,600 in senior secondary schools ("Bachillerato"); and 1,246,795 in universities, teachers's colleges and other post-secondary institutions. The remaining students were either in kindergarten or in technical and on-the-job apprenticeships.[3]

The history of educational policy in Mexico is deeply intertwined with the history of the Mexican Revolution. The abolition of illiteracy and the development of a system of universal public education, accessible to all, was a central goal of the new revolutionary government. Article Three of the Constitution set out the right of every citizen to free, accessible and publicly provided education.

During the decades immediately following the revolution in 1910, Mexico became a leader in the development of populist education programs. Enormous strides were taken, especially during the 1930s and 1940s to provide educational opportunities to the peasantry.

In the period after World War II, the educational system continued to expand rapidly in response to the high expectations which had been created by the revolution. The governing party was committed to higher spending on education. This was seen as the key to achieving Mexico's social, cultural and economic development.

By 1980, the level of illiteracy had been dramatically reduced, despite rapid population growth, limited resources and continuing widespread poverty.

Illiteracy Rates in Mexico, 1980

Age	Male	Female
15 years old or less	14.1%	17.8%
15 — 24	5.8%	7.4%
25-44	11.4%	18.1%
45 and Older	22.8%	32.9%

Source: Mexico Ministry of Education

Between 1921 and 1990 the rate of illiteracy dropped from 66 per cent to an estimated 6 per cent. The percentage of Mexicans able to attend primary school increased from 22 per cent to 98 per cent according to the Ministry of Education. While this figure may overstate the success of the country's educational system in addressing the problem of illiteracy, there is no question of the real progress achieved in this area.

While major strides were taken in the primary and secondary levels in the early postwar period, more recently there has been very rapid growth in higher education. In 1960, there were 76,000 undergraduates and 350 graduates in the system.

By 1985, this had increased to 1,107,000 undergraduates and 37,000 graduates. And in 1991, the figures were 1,201,849 and 44,946 respectively.[4]

The growth in students was paralleled by a corresponding growth in institutions from 31 in 1960 to 763 in 1991. It was also accompanied by the rapid expansion of facilities and student numbers in the regions outside Mexico City. Whereas over half the total of undergraduate students lived in Mexico City in 1970, by 1991 less than a quarter were studying in the capital.

Over the past 30 years, there has been a notable 'democratization' of access to higher education in Mexico, with 1 in 40 of the 20-24 age group attending post-secondary education in 1960 compared to 1 in 7 by 1985. And the number of women has increased from 26.3 per cent in 1977 to 41.6 per cent in 1991 (excluding enrolment in teachers' colleges).

The system of education in Mexico has been — and remains — overwhelmingly public at all levels. In 1991, 80.7 per cent of undergraduates and 78.9 per cent of graduate students attended public institutions.[5]

Highly Centralized

At the primary and secondary level, the Mexican education system has been highly centralized, with the national government playing the dominant role in funding, paying teachers' salaries and overseeing curriculum development.

This centralized system reflected the high national priority given to education throughout the post-revolutionary period when the major goal was to provide peasants and workers with basic education and reduce illiteracy. Educating the masses was seen as a task which only the central government had the resources to fulfil. One of the key benefits of this approach was to equalize educational opportunities across the country, ensuring that even the poorest states could provide a minimal standard of schooling for children within their jurisdiction.

Another objective of education in Mexico was to provide the population with the skills needed for the country's modernization program. Since the revolution, Mexico has tried to chart a path to economic development based on the development of its domestic industry. Foreign-controlled firms were excluded from many sectors of the economy. Other sectors were reserved for state corporations to prevent foreign takeovers. There was a strong component of self-reliance. Policies were formulated to prevent Mexico from being drawn into a branch-plant relationship with the United States. This approach to industrial development required an educational system which provided the skills and training for a domestically-controlled, relatively diversified manufacturing sector, much of which was publicly owned.

The development of Mexico's educational system has followed a somewhat different path from that taken by Canada (and the U.S. for that matter). Education has been seen as fundamental to the nation's economic development plans. The national government, which has been the formulator of these plans, has played a dominant role, with lower levels of government having a much smaller part in the establishment and administration of the system. Given Mexico's development needs, the priority given by the federal government to building the educational system can be seen as a logical and effective approach to economic and social, as well as educational, advancement.

The Growth Of Teachers' Unions

One of the other major consequences of a centralized, national system of education, funded by the federal government, has been to give the national teachers' union a major role in the shaping of educational policy and the allocation of educational resources. The National Union of Education Workers (SNTE) represents the vast majority of primary, secondary and some post-secondary teachers. Like other unions in Mexico, it has had a close relationship with the governing Institutional Revolutionary Party (PRI) and the Ministry of Public Education almost since the union was founded 49 years ago. The government has consulted with it on most matters related to educational policy for over two generations. Indeed, the teachers' union could be described as an integral part of Mexico's educational establishment.

The dominant role of the national government in education funding and curriculum development has made it possible for the SNTE to represent teachers throughout the country. Consequently, the union has been able to organize and represent almost a million educational workers at the national level in collective bargaining and in policy discussions with the government.[6]

At the same time the union has also been deeply influenced by its affiliation to the governing party, the PRI, which has ruled Mexico since the revolution. The influence is so strong that senior officials in the union ended up being chosen by the PRI. Indeed, some would see the union as having frequently acted as a *de facto* representative of the Ministry of Public Education, supporting its policies and using its influence with teachers to assist the government in implementing educational programs. Between 1949 and 1989, the union had only two leaders: Jesus Robles Martinez (1949-72) and Carlos Jonguitud Barrios (1972-89), giving rise to charges of 'bossism' and undemocratic practices.[7]

Over the past 10 years — and particularly since President Salinas took power — there has been growing opposition within the SNTE to its cosy relationship to the PRI and the policies of the education ministry.[8] In 1989, there was a three-week wildcat strike involving more than half a million teachers organized by dissidents in the teachers' union. This led to the ousting of Barrios. It also led to calls for a basic change in the political direction of the teachers' union.[9]

The SNTE now has a very active reform caucus called the National Coordination of Education Workers which is pushing to democratize the union, end its dominance by PRI appointees and encourage it to operate more independently of the government, so that it can act as a national voice for the interests of teachers and the broader public educational system in Mexico.[10]

The new activism in the teachers' union can be seen, in part, as a reaction to the sweeping proposals for educational change which are being pushed through by the Salinas government. They can also be seen as a response to the diminution of the role of the union in shaping Mexican educational policy.

Mexico's Debt Crisis And The Shift To 'Free Market' Policies

The economic crisis of 1982 precipitated a dramatic change in the system of education in Mexico. Pressured by international bankers and the IMF's restructuring regime, the cash-strapped

Mexican government initiated a massive series of cuts to educational funding — cuts which were implemented largely through deliberately allowing inflation to erode the real value of teachers' salaries.[11] Adjusted for inflation, salaries have fallen by between 50 and 60 per cent over the past decade. The crisis also led to a reduction in the demand for graduates and the temporary 'saturation' of the labour market for professionals in many fields.

These specific changes to the education system were reinforced by the broader economic and political policies initiated by the PRI since 1982. The government turned its back on the tradition of 'statism' in Mexico and decided to open up the economy to international competition. This meant reducing the size and role of the central government so that market forces and foreign investors could operate more freely. It meant a massive program of privatization of public enterprises.

It meant joining the GATT in 1985 (for the first time in Mexico's history). This decision also entailed a wide variety of commitments to open Mexico's economy further to international market forces.[12] And, most recently, it meant consolidating this entire free market agenda through negotiating NAFTA, thus locking Mexico into a new economic framework which would permanently close the door on Mexico's previous economic development strategy.

The decision to unleash international market forces in the Mexican economy has profoundly affected the organization, funding, curriculum and structure of education in Mexico in the very short period since the 'reforms' were begun in 1982 and particularly since President Salinas came to office in 1988.

The new economy requires a different skills mix. Instead of training for a self-reliant, protected manufacturing sector, the new economy will be dominated by branch plants of U.S. multinational companies. Marketing, business administration and a host of new service occupations will be needed, while many of the traditional skills needed to operate a diversified domestic manufacturing industry or run Mexico's (previously) large number of state enterprises will no longer be in demand.[13]

One of the most important developments in the restructuring of education has been the Salinas government's push to decentralize the administration of the public educational system. Although this policy had been officially adopted by earlier administrations, for almost a decade its implementation had been successfully frustrated by oppositon forces. However, in the past two years, Salinas has succeeded in pushing it through. The government's policy will break apart the national system of education. Each of the 31 states will now be responsible for running the educational programs within its jurisdiction. There will also be a separate system for the federal district of Mexico City. The national system will thus fragment into 32 separately administered local systems.

Funding will also be 'downloaded', with individual states being required to pick up an increasingly greater share of the costs formerly paid by the national government. (It is notable that these 'reforms' parallel the policy of the U.S. federal government under Reagan and Bush of abandoning the federal government's fiscal responsibility for education. There are equally clear parallels with the Mulroney government's throttling of Established Programs Financing (EPF) transfers to the provinces.)

However, while responsibility for the operation and, increasingly, the funding of education will be 'downloaded' to the states, curriculum decisions will remain centralized, and a new curriculum is already being put in place.

Another 'reform' Salinas has introduced is a change in the federal government's attitude toward private religious schools. Since the revolution, Mexico has been quite hostile to the Catholic Church, seeing it as a force for reaction. It is only very recently that Mexico has sought to open up diplomatic links with the Vatican. As part of his efforts to weaken the public system, Salinas has opened the door to private confessional schools to offer primary and secondary education in competition with state schools. It remains to be seen whether this change will result in a dramatic increase in religious educational enrolment. But the intention of the government in making this change is clear: end the dominance of the state-controlled primary and secondary schools and open the door to private education.

Splitting Up Collective Bargaining

The downloading of administrative responsibility to individual states also has major repercussions for the wages and working conditions of teachers. After extensive and difficult negotiations, the Salinas government signed an accord with the SNTE in May of 1992. The National Agreement to Modernize Basic Education addressed the impact of the break-up of the federal system on the wages and working conditions of teachers, making provisions for the transition to the new state-administered systems and providing for a wage increase of 20 per cent to facilitate the transition. (Even so, the wages of teachers will still average only $13 (Cdn) per day.)

The agreement also provides for the development of new educational materials to reflect Mexico's changing social, economic and political situation.[14] This was a key goal of the Salinas government.

The teachers' union will be broken up into 32 locals, while still having some recognition as a national union. However, the terms and conditions of employment of teachers will now fall under the jurisdiction of each state government. Within a week after the signing of the agreement, 15 of the state governments had moved unilaterally, without consulting the teachers, to amend their laws and establish new state education committees to oversee school administration. In these states, the employment status of teachers was also changed — unilaterally — by making them state employees.[15]

While the long-term consequences of this decentralization are not yet clear, it is likely that the teachers' union's influence on future education policy will be dramatically reduced. This appears to be one of the goals of the Salinas government in pushing decentralization. Teacher resources and the focus of teacher organizing will now be concentrated on individual states, rather than at the federal level. The union may simply fragment into a loose federation of state-based locals unable to focus significant resources on issues of national education policy.[16] According to one observer:

> The agreement signed by the governors and by the National Union of Educational Workers (SNTE) signifies the beginning

of the end of this union....[17]

Conditions of employment and school resources for teachers may well deteriorate in the poorer states due to the withdrawal of federal funds and the eventual abandonment of the national pay grid. The lack of resources at the state level is likely to result in policies of wage restraint. Inequalities in resources allocated by states will grow, reflecting the varying levels of economic development in different parts of the country.

The education policies of the Salinas government have already precipitated a number of major protests by teachers. The recent agreement was met by demonstrations by pre-school and primary school teachers in Mexico City. Aside from protesting the negative consequences of localized salary negotiations, the teachers declared that the agreement will open the door to greater privatization of the educational system.[18]

There are also major concerns about the future of educational services to indigenous peoples within Mexico. In one state, Oaxaca, the teachers recently staged a hunger strike near the state governor's palace to protest the elimination of the 21-year-old Indigenous Education program.[19]

The Implications Of Decentralization

A reduced federal role in education parallels other changes introduced throughout the Mexican economy. In 1990, the Mexican Constitution was amended to end one of the key reforms of the Mexican revolution: publicly-owned farmland (*ejidos*) which provided the basis of the co-operative farms. It has been estimated, conservatively, that this change, coupled with opening up the Mexican corn market to cheap U.S. imports, may displace over 600,000 farmers.[20] In 1991, the entire banking system was privatized. A wide variety of state enterprises were sold off to private investors, including the telephone system, the state airlines and state-owned manufacturing and transportation operations.

According to Hugo Aboites of the National Autonomous University of Mexico, the decentralization of education should be viewed in the context of this privatization and commercialization of Mexican society:

A decentralized educational system, for example, allows private groups to have a greater influence in the curriculum and on the supervision of how tax money is spent in education. Although the decentralization has been presented as a way of increasing public participation on the education (sic) at the local and state level, the real intentions can be considered much more specific if one attends to other facts.

In 1990, for example, the Ministry of Public Education and the national representatives of the business community signed an agreement which allows for full private participation in the revision of study plans of middle and higher public education, participation in school boards and a greater integration of school to industry. It refers to all education directly under the control of the Ministry, but it also represents a very strong signal of the government's intentions to institutions of higher education that are autonomous. With these changes, Mexican education moves to equate with its U.S. counterpart, [the] symbol of modernization.[21]

Selling Free Trade: Rewriting Mexico's History

As noted earlier, there has been a major official rewriting of Mexico's history to accommodate and justify current neo-liberal policies. At the direction of President Salinas, a new pro-American, pro-business version of Mexico's development is now being taught in the 4th, 5th and 6th years of primary school.

The Mexican Constitution requires that the government provide a set of official texts which schools throughout the country must use. These texts are distributed free within the public school system. Teachers are obliged to use them and cannot substitute other texts.

The system pre-dates Salinas' administration. After the revolution, the government felt the need to provide a standardized curriculum to ensure that its new educational policies were implemented. A centralized curriculum also provided a much needed resource to rural schools who would not themselves have the capacity to develop their own material. In recent years, however, teachers have questioned the constraints associated with having 'official' versions of history imposed on the schools, while alternative interpretations are exluded. But, the Salinas government has taken this tradition much further by ordering that the study of history (i.e., official history) be given much greater prominence. The political — indeed ideological — importance of this measure cannot be overstated, as most Mexicans do not study history beyond primary school.

These three new texts, according to the major teachers' union, are rife with factual errors, as well as being biased and unashamedly pro-Salinas throughout. Such was the opposition among historians, teachers and academics that Salinas was forced to withdraw the texts temporarily while a commission he appointed studied the matter.[22]

The history texts contain a totally different version of the 20th-century history of Mexico than their predecessors. The repressive pre-1910 dictatorship of Porfirio Diaz, which provoked the Mexican revolution, is treated sympathetically. Diaz is portrayed as a modernizer and an economic rationalist who understood the need for business development and for a more balanced approach towards relations with the United States.

Diaz's vicious repression of indigenous peoples, campesinos and labour unions is ignored. And his more favourable attitude towards U.S. business interests is portrayed as a virtue, rather than an indication of toadying to foreign interests.

Many of the achievements of the Mexican revolution are downplayed. The massive effort to eliminate illiteracy and to develop popular education during the 1930s an 1940s is largely ignored. The remarkable growth of Mexico's economy under the nationalist approach favoured by earlier PRI governments is dismissed as antiquated and backward.

More recent historical events have received an equally convenient rewrite. The enormous controversy over the 1988 election — which many believe Salinas won only by massive electoral fraud — is ignored. Instead, it is simply noted that he received 52 per cent of the vote. Even the names of the opposition candidates are left out. However, there is lots of space in the new texts to make numerous favourable references to Salinas and the education minister, endorsing the soundness of their economic and social policies.

In short, Salinas' concern to consolidate his economic changes has led him to rewrite Mexico's history to justify his current economic and social policies.

Higher Education In Mexico

Higher education in Mexico has evolved in a somewhat different manner than the primary and secondary educational system. Universities in Mexico have placed a high priority on their independence from the state and have struggled to limit the direct interference of successive PRI governments over the past 70 years in their internal affairs.[23] This conflict was most acute in the 1920s and 1930s around the role of the state in the funding and governance of the National Autonomous University of Mexico.[24]

At the same time, there has been an ongoing pattern of attempts by governments to shape the development of the university system, both through controlling university purse strings and through the creation of new institutions designed to achieve specific governmental objectives with respect to training and economic development.

In the post-World War II period, Mexico's universities have played a somewhat contradictory role in the political system. They have been both the source of education for the governing elite of the PRI and the focus of opposition to the policies of the government. From the 1940s to the late 1960s, the number of private universities grew substantially, and their enrolment expanded to about 15 per cent of the total student population. Perhaps more significantly, private universities came to exercise a disproportionate influence in the training of Mexico's governing elite, while the public institutions have been a major source of pressure for egalitarian reforms.[25]

In the 1960s, Mexico's public universities underwent major changes. Enrolment increased substantially. A student movement emerged, partly influenced by the increasing numbers of children of newly-prosperous skilled workers, government employees, artisans and small business people. During the 1970s, the government sought to rebuild the trust that had been shattered by the government-initiated massacre at Tlaltelolco in 1968. Public funds to universities were dramatically increased from 23 per cent of operating budgets in 1970 to 70 per cent by 1980.

Aside from the enormous expansion which the new money facilitated, universities witnessed other major changes. The cumulative effects of these changes have been summarized by Aboites:

> Thus, by the end of the seventies, Mexican public university (sic) was postulated as an *autonomous* institution, administrated and governed by the *universitatios* (university community) themselves, with the exclusion of the state and the corporations in the university affairs. It was *democratic*, both in the sense of the purposes of its participatory system of governance and of its role in fostering wider civil participation through education. It was *progressive* in as much as it attempted to establish alternative interpretations regarding society and which gave an important role to the social perspectives arising from peasant and workers interests. *Tuition-free* and *massive*, it was portrayed as a road of social mobility. Finally, *professionalised*, as university workers insisted that its contribution to society was to be based on the work of a permanent number of full-time faculty and staff, fully integrated to the main processes of institutional life.[26]

Restructuring Higher Education

Since the debt crisis of the mid-1980s and through the Salinas presidency, Mexico's public universities have been subjected to major funding cuts. This has led to pressures to increase tuition and abandon the commitment to unrestricted universal access. Mexico's National Autonomous University has 270,000 students, largely as a result of the open admissions policy. However, it has not received the funds necessary to ensure that its facilities and programs keep pace with its enrolment. As one commentator recently noted:

> ... [T]he proud centrepiece of Mexico's educational system is going broke. Its sprawling University City campus, decorated by priceless mosaic works by Diego Rivera and other famous Mexican artists, is run-down and shabby.
>
> The peso pinch shows: The library is missing crucial volumes, young adults sit at 30-year-old desks designed for grammar-school students, and maintenance cutbacks have left some buildings filthy and unsafe. Teachers are leaving in droves, because salaries are frozen and inflation is not....
>
> The alarming decline and the federal government's refusal to raise subsidies have forced the administration to gingerly

propose a steep tuition hike, perhaps to $400 (US). In protest, students are taking to the streets to claim that their constitutional right to free education is being violated.[27]

The squeeze on university funding has meant that the salaries of professors have fallen by an estimated 50 per cent to 60 per cent in real terms since the early 1980s.[28] Teachers are increasingly moving to private universities or to jobs in private industry as a result of the unattractive salaries now being paid.

The funding crisis has also precipitated a major debate about the constitutional rights of Mexicans. Article Three of the Constitution gave every Mexican the right to a free education as part of the 80-year-old revolution's commitment to improving the lot of workers and campesinos. While universities do charge tuition fees, in recent years their real value has fallen to 200 pesos (10 cents) a year, which many see as effectively being free. Thus proposals to resolve the fiscal crisis of the universities by dramatically raising tuition fees are interpreted as attempts to move the system in an exclusive, elitist direction.[29]

Linked with its restructuring agenda, in 1984 the government took the first steps towards securing centralized control over the courses offered at universities. This has been done through a carrot-and-stick approach: research grants and salary bonuses are selectively given to academics working in areas the government sees as commercially worthwhile. And they are deliberately withheld from those carrying out research which has no obvious economic applications.

Merit System On A Lever

A merit system now allocates federal government resources to areas which the government believes are vital for Mexico's modernization. This system was adopted as an alternative to a general increase in the salaries of university teachers.[30] It thus gives the government a major financial lever to control university work.

Under the program, qualifying academics were initially given tax-free merit increases of between 1 and 5 times the basic monthly salary. This translated into an increase in annual earnings of up to 50 per cent. Recently, the amounts have been increased to between 3 and 9 times the minimum academic salary. In practice, this means that professors can earn up to 90 per cent, or more, above their salaries if they carry out research which the government sees as economically useful.

The lever of control is that the funds are administered not by the universities, but directly by the education ministry.[31] While those who are recipients of the merit pay are generally supportive of the system, it has come in for serious criticism from excluded professors whose disciplines (liberal arts, generally) have been seen as arbitrarily having been excluded. However, the government is intent on pressing on with this approach, as it believes that the universities must focus more of their talent and resources on disciplines and research which will make Mexico more competitive in the global economy.

The government has also pushed the universities to establish stronger linkages with corporations.[32] Under this new policy, universities are being encouraged to work with the private sector with the goal of strengthening Mexico's competitive position.

This new relationship was summarized in a comment made by the Under-Secretary of Higher Education and Scientific Research of the Ministry of Education and quoted in *La Jornada*:

> The most important part of the new university will be its linkage to society…; joint planning between universities and industry; sharing of information for decision making; coordinated use of laboratories of industry, coordinated research, and that industry's training and professionalization of its personnel become a process (endorsed) by the certification of the universities.[33]

The Salinas government has pushed the universities into making alliances with business through making programs and funding contingent on reaching agreements with industry and through involving senior business executives on the National Council for Science and Technology which oversees the government's policy development for scientific and technical training.[34]

A Move To Standardize Accreditation

As part of the Salinas government's restructuring of education, a U.S. consulting organization, the International Council for Educational Development, was recently commissioned to draft recommendations on the reform of Mexico's system of higher education. Aside from commenting on the very low salaries paid to Mexican academics (less than $500 (US) per month, on average), the report recommended the establishment of a national system of accreditation overseen by a proposed national accreditation agency. Its purpose would be to set uniform standards for higher education in Mexico.[35]

Both the consultants and the Mexican government recognize that this proposal will generate a great deal of opposition from Mexican universities, which cherish their autonomy and resent government interference in academic matters. Concern has already been expressed by some academics that reforms should not be accompanied by political interference.[36]

In sum, Mexico's system of public higher education is being fundamentally transformed. The purpose is to 'modernize' — a term which really means to commercialize and privatize. The growing involvement of business at all levels in Mexican education and the willingness of the current government to restructure the system according to the demands of multinational corporations for a suitably-trained workforce are clearly part of the free trade agenda.

Mexico's tradition of public education is being systematically undermined by a government which is committed to elite private education, focused on the needs of the upper and middle classes. The outcome will be a dual educational system in which 'public' means substandard and 'private' means affluent and well resourced. It will move Mexico in the direction of the U.S. system, where cash-starved, inner-city public schools coexist with well-heeled suburban institutions.

The recent experience of Mexico has disturbing parallels with developments in Canada and, as we shall see below, with trends in other parts of Latin America.

The Broader Context Of Market Reforms

The economic, social and educational changes happening in Mexico have to be seen in the context of developments in the rest of Latin America. This is particularly important given the quite explicit intention of the U.S. government to expand the NAFTA to other countries in Central and South America through the Accession clause in the deal. Indeed, the issue of free trade agreements is at the top of the economic agenda of virtually every country in the Americas.

Noel McGinn, a leading scholar on Mexican and Latin American educational systems, has suggested that the new free trade deals being negotiated between the U.S., Mexico and other Latin American countries will lead to important changes to existing educational systems throughout the hemisphere.

Free-market economic policies will be the driving force behind these changes. Multinational corporations are already demanding that national educational systems be reshaped throughout Latin America to meet their growing labour needs:

> Increased pressure for 'relevance' in curriculum will mean greater emphasis on skills that can be 'sold' in the labour marketplace. That will mean a reduction in teaching of classics, languages other than those used in the 'business world' (specifically reduced teaching of French), geography and history, physical education and the arts. The beneficiaries will be mathematics, science, and applied language (i.e. reading, comprehension, business writing, but not creative writing).[37]

McGinn believes that, under free trade, governments will be under enormous pressure to adopt new national and international standards designed to make it easier for corporations to measure what students have learned, thereby enabling them to recruit workers with the desired skills, knowledge and attitudes. Forced to compete with other countries for capital, national governments will experience growing pressure to provide corporations with workers who have competitive labour skills.[38] And they will restructure their educational programs to meet this perceived need.

Pushing Towards Private Schools

Due to the imposition and likely continuance of austerity measures by the IMF, World Bank and other international financial bodies; due to population growth; due to the need to service their international debts and due to the pressure to reduce taxation and public spending, financially strapped Third-World governments will end up spending less on public education. Teacher salaries, school construction, equipment and other educational 'inputs' will be under very severe constraints in the public system. National governments will continue to download educational costs to less well-financed state and local governments.

This will happen at precisely the same time that curriculum decisions will become increasingly centralized at the national level in response to economic pressures on governments to provide transnational corporations with a suitably-educated labour force.

The lack of funding for public education will result in a growing demand for elite private education. This tendency will be encouraged by the expanding opportunities for highly educated workers who, under free trade, will be able to work in other countries, pursuing international careers with multinational corporations. New and expanding private educational institutions will rapidly become the vehicles through which aspiring upper- and upper-middle-class students acquire the appropriate languages, technical skills and connections to pursue the new careers which free trade will open up to a select group within Latin-American societies.[39]

McGinn argues that the transnational corporations have not only pressured governments to begin restructuring the public educational system: they have already taken steps to promote a rapid expansion of private education in Latin America. This is because it has proven to be much more amenable to their demands for a business-oriented curriculum.[40]

Free trade has other implications for Mexico and other Latin-American countries. With respect to the public educational systems, McGinn suggests that there will be growing pressures to achieve both national and international harmonization of standards throughout the new common market:

[N]ational systems could develop external examinations to measure the competence (knowledge, skills and attitudes) of graduates. Over time the content of these examinations would be standardized across the countries in the union. This approach is likely to be favoured by the transnationals, to ensure the quality of labour across countries.[41]

At the post-secondary level, there are already calls for an 'academic common market' by a number of university administrators. This would, however, be very different than earlier and much smaller-scale bilateral and multilateral exchanges within Latin America. These have often been organized with the goal of limiting or excluding the influence of the U.S. and thus protect national institutions.

Instead, this new 'common market' approach would allow U.S. educational institutions to play a central role. And it would permit U.S.-based transnational corporations to provide much of the financial and organization support.

European Experience Is Different

The path of educational harmonization under free trade within Latin America will, most likely, be quite different from the experience of Western Europe. In the European Community (EC) there has been a conscious effort to promote educational co-operation and, where feasible, the harmonization of standards.[42] Yet, despite a great deal of interest and effort, educational integration in Europe has been very slow and largely a result of accommodation to very specific economic reforms and, more generally, to the EC's policy of labour mobility:

> Economic integration has been a major stimulus to major changes in some aspects of the education and training systems of the European Community countries. Education has been changed most where it interfaces directly with the economy, in technical education and job training at the secondary level, and in professional training at the university level.[43]

Harmonization has been slowed by what many would see as a sensible policy of respecting national, cultural and historic traditions with respect to curriculum, governance, administration and funding. Non-economic considerations have, quite consciously, been given a very high priority. Change purely for economic reasons has been limited to areas where economic forces were most pressing. It has also been impeded by the obvious difficulties in getting all member states to agree — a problem compounded by the political sensitivity of educational issues.

However, the free trade agreements which the U.S. is pushing to implement throughout Latin America have no similar commitments to national sovereignty, democratic input or the historic role of educational stakeholders in the member countries. Quite the contrary, they are designed to limit the power of governments, while enhancing the power of the market to shape future educational decisions throughout the hemisphere. According to McGinn:

> The European countries that formed the initial community were relatively equally balanced in terms of population, size of economy, and distribution of income. Most of the countries had national labour unions that were major actors in all political decisions. Social and political equality does not hold in the Americas, and as a consequence, decision making based on economic market forces alone will favour powerful financial interests in the U.S. in alliance with their counterparts in the poorer countries, to the detriment of ordinary citizens in both places.[44]

Once the new trade agreements are in place, the role of national governments in formulating educational policy — whether in Mexico or in the future signatories to NAFTA — will be circumscribed by the provisions of the trade deals. Mexico and the other countries of Latin America will be under intense pressure to restructure their economies — and their education and training programs — to entice multinational corporations to invest. Failure to provide a suitably-trained labour force will raise the spectre of capital going elsewhere at precisely the same time that formerly protected domestic industries are threatened with extinction from the new, tariff-free environment created by the trade deal.

All of this brings us back to the transformation of the Mexican educational system. The corporations have a very clear agenda: they want Mexico to provide them with a labour force which has the skills and work habits needed to carry out a dramatic expansion of their production facilities. They need major changes in Mexico's educational system to ensure that this happens.

Under Salinas, they have a government which is willing to do this as a way of attracting foreign capital, and as a strategy of burying the past and consolidating the so-called 'reforms' which he has introduced.

The influence of teachers, academics, students, unions and local communities will be replaced by that of big business. Public educational objectives which do not support commercial objectives will be downgraded or abandoned. Control of curriculum will become even more centralized, while the federal government's role in financing will diminish.

In sum, the changes which NAFTA are likely to bring about in the Mexican education system are not those optimistically portrayed by Canada's former International Trade Minister Michael Wilson: those of facilitating Mexico's modernization process and permitting Mexico to move out of its Third-World position to that of a developed economy. Rather, they are changes which will see the subordination of education policy — much of which has been very progressive — to the needs of multinational capital.

A Note On The Deficit In High-Tech Trade

The federal government has maintained that Mexico poses no threat to Canadian jobs and Canadian industry because it will be exporting low value-added products based on low-skill, labour intensive production. Canada, according to Michael Wilson, will be exporting high value-added products based on our better educated and trained labour force.

However, a recent study of Canada's trade with Mexico by Nuala Beck has found that the Canadian government's assumptions about the composition of trade with Mexico is wrong. The main problem Canada will have in its trade with Mexico is not in dealing with a flood of labour intensive goods such as textiles, but rather in terms of sophisticated, high value-added products.

Beck analyzed the labour content in Canada's import and export trade with Mexico. The results show that Canada is being "blown out of the water" in high-knowledge intensive trade with Mexico:

> The big surprise for (Trade Minister) Michael Wilson's office and ourselves is seeing the amount of high-knowledge goods that are coming from Mexico. Our analysis shows that for every $1 of high-knowledge intensive goods that we exported to Mexico last year, we imported $7.67" (*Vancouver Sun*, October 9, 1992).

Beck went on to say that Canada's trade position in high-knowledge goods was deteriorating at an alarming rate. Canada's imports of moderate- and high-knowledge products from Mexico jumped from $1.38 billion in 1990 to $2.17 billion in 1991. Of these, $411 million were high-knowledge intensity imports and $1.76 million were moderate-knowledge imports. In contrast, Mexico bought only $242 million in moderate and high-knowledge Canadian exports in 1991. And this represented a sharp decline of almost $100 million from the previous year.

Beck's findings quickly make sense once we understand that the new factories being put in Mexico are not primarily low-technology textile and leather factories but advanced auto, computer, electronics and chemical factories. These facilities, especially in the Maquiladoras area, have been built as export platforms, using the most advanced technology to produce for the U.S. and Canadian markets. In short, it is not Mexico which is exporting to Canada; it is the large multinational corporations who have located facilities in Mexico which are exporting to Canada.

Chapter Five

The 'Americanization' of Canadian Education

No one should be surprised to learn that free trade between the U.S. and Canada is not just in goods and services, but also in ideology. But the trade in ideas is mostly one-way. This increases pressure to make Canada's school system follow the current trends in the U.S. toward business goals and privatization.

The U.S. and Canada have historically had significantly different ideas about the role of public education in meeting social and cultural objectives. In the U.S., public education was seen, through the common school, as a key institution in taming the polyglot of immigrants and creating the 'American'. Individualism and the equal opportunity to change social class through individual effort in the free enterprise system was to replace group identification with the culture and the social identity of the 'old country'.

Canada's public schools, on the other hand, reflect an institutionalization of differences. The governance of schools and the content of curriculum were built on a recognition of the rights of cultural groups. Thus, across the country one still finds separate, but public, school systems based on religion and/or language. Even British Columbia, which resisted pressure for separate public schools for over a century, started funding private religious and elite schools in the 1970s, and is about to set up a separate francophone public school board.

With these significant differences in social purpose, one would think that the FTA and NAFTA would represent little threat to the Canadian public school system. Such is not the case.

In both countries, social and cultural objectives are increasingly being subjugated to the *economic*. While culture may seem to be fragmenting into smaller units, the conventional wisdom is that the economy is becoming more globally integrated. When economic aspects of education become central, the scene is set for 'harmonization' of the school systems.

Harmonization will have a downward impact on public education in Canada in at least four areas: pressure to decrease the level of funding to education; reduction in social programs that improve the quality of the lives of children; demands to limit collective bargaining rights of teachers; and pressure to open delivery of education services to privatization and 'market solutions'.

Each of these will be examined in some detail, but first it is important to see the ideologies and strategies that produce this downward pressure. Michael Wilson, the person who, until recently, was in charge of Canada's negotiation of NAFTA, has claimed that education is exempt from the agreement. However, the ideology and power relations that have produced NAFTA are already having an impact on public education in Canada, and will continue to even if NAFTA is never ratified by the United States.

Although the U.S. and Canada don't share the same history, they do share many of the same transnationals. The Chief Executive Officers (CEOs) of Canadian branches of transnationals put the real push behind the FTA and then NAFTA. These same CEOs have set up copy-cat organizations in Canada to serve as platforms of influence on public policy. And it is these same CEOs who are defining the corporate agenda in Canadian education — an agenda that incorporates the themes espoused by their U.S. counterparts (and bosses) in the Business Roundtable and the Business Higher Education Forum and enunciated in reports such as former President Bush's America 2000. These reports aim to make the corporate agenda seem like 'common sense' by repeating it so many times in so many ways.

Two of the copy-cat Canadian business organizations are following the model defined by the Roundtable in the United States. The Business Council on National Issues (BCNI) was established in 1976, a few years after the Roundtable. Like the Roundtable, the BCNI is made up of the CEOs of the major 'Canadian' corporations. Canadian business leaders emulated the approach taken by the Roundtable, which is based on direct, personal lobbying of government by top business leaders. They chose to avoid the more public forms of lobbying that characterized some of the other business organizations and instead wield their rather substantial power behind the scenes.[1]

Rather than waiting to react to government issues, the BCNI takes pre-emptive positions based on extensive research and containing specific recommendations, often already drafted as laws. Using this approach, it "tries to set the overall framework or direction of state policy."[2]

By 1985, the BCNI adopted the agenda for free trade negotiations with the U.S., not only influencing Canadian politicians, but also meeting with key officials in the American government and securing "the endorsement of their counterparts in the Business Roundtable. The two organizations agreed to cooperate in seeking a fair, balanced agreement between two countries, [and] urged that the negotiations be moved in such a way that an agreement can be achieved expeditiously."[3]

More recently, the BCNI commissioned a $1.5-million study by Harvard University's Michael Porter (with most of the cost picked up by the Canadian taxpayers, courtesy of the federal government). What did Porter suggest in his report? In regard to education, he repeated the conventional wisdom in the corporate community: create national educational standards; have provincial governments agree to testing mechanisms to meet the standards; put more emphasis on science, math and technology and transform the universities into institutions to promote economic development.[4]

Another organization which has adopted an approach similar to the Business Roundtable is the Conference Board of Canada. Education policy has been a major thrust of the work of the Conference Board. While other such corporate groups have committees that work on education policy issues, the

Conference Board has created a subsidiary — the National Business and Education Centre — with its own secretariat and researchers.

The purpose of the Centre is "to help (sic) business and education leaders work collaboratively to promote the development of an education system that will prepare Canada's youth for tomorrow's world."[5] An examination of reports from the Centre repeat the common themes.

One of them is partnership. The Centre has held annual conferences on business-education partnerships to allow business leaders to bring their message directly to education decision-makers. Typical of the content was a keynote speech by W.N. Kissick, CEO at Union Carbide (a petrochemical transnational corporation), at the 1990 conference. Kissick made the claim that Canada is next to the top in resources for education and near the bottom in results on science and math. He called for national goals and testing, and promoted Bush's six goals for education.

Kissick also called, again, for business-education partnerships. Interestingly, one reason that he gave for needing partnerships was that business had lost the dominant position that it had once held on school boards, where "there was a direct business influence on curricula and standards." Businessmen and professionals have been replaced, he said, by "organized parent and community groups."[6]

Selling The "Skills Profile"

The other major project of the National Business and Education Centre is the development of an "employability skills profile." The purpose of the project was to create a common agenda of expectations that business has of the schools. The plan was to consult widely with elite groups in business education and equity groups. The profile was then to be widely distributed, providing content for lobbying by business people with decision-makers.

But the Centre actually built its skills profile on the Michigan Employability Skills Profile. It then called together people from business, labour and education in several "reaction groups" across the country, publishing a revised final result and distributing it widely. Although it makes reference to "other goals and objectives" of the school, the focus on students as future workers is clear.[7] Its skill list is aimed at having elementary and secondary schools develop competencies in students to "maximize their productivity, participation and personal satisfaction when they enter the workplace; and to meet the current and future needs of employers for skilled entry-level employees."[8]

An example of the success of this strategy was illustrated when one of the associate deputy ministers in B.C.'s education ministry handed out at meetings the Conference Board's profile of employability skills as a key document around which the ministry's communication strategy should be built.

Another similar group bringing the corporate agenda to education is the Corporate-Higher Education Forum. It is made up of both corporate CEOs and university presidents. It, too, has connections with the BCNI. The BCNI president, Thomas d'Aquino, is an associate member.

Although much of its work relates to building corporate influence over the universities, it also has held conferences with a focus on the elementary and secondary systems, and published a report called "To Be Our Best: Learning for the Future." It contains all the familiar proposals, including a long list of suggestions for business-school partnerships.[9]

A full list of business efforts to influence education policy to meet the demand for 'global competitiveness' would be quite long. Recent reports of this sort include Focus 2000: Report on the Task Force on Education and Training from the Canadian Chamber of Commerce (1989); Learning to Win: Education, Training and National Prosperity from the National Advisory Board on Science and Technology (1991); and A Lot to Learn, from the now-defunct Economic Council of Canada.

The themes and recommendations become a mantra as one reads report after report: national goals; system performance assessments against the goals; strong emphasis on science, math and technology; business-education partnerships.

Chanting Global Competitiveness

The mantra is amplified as well by the media that particularly targets the business community as its audience. A recent content analysis of education coverage in the *Globe and Mail* found that the *Globe* articles "tend to follow the agenda of business critics" and frames issues in ways that exclude "individuals and groups, including unions, which may have a contrary view on national standards or may take a position that different priorities than the issue of national standards are important to the education system."[10]

Business and the business press are not alone in the global competitiveness mantra. Provincial government commissions, task forces and 'summits' all play the same theme. They range across the political and geographic map, from New Brunswick with Premier Frank McKenna's Commission on Excellence in Education to British Columbia and Premier Mike Harcourt's June, 1993 summit with business and labour on training and skills.

The most significant government chanters of the competitiveness mantra, however, are at the national level. Centrepieces of the policy, of course, have been the FTA and NAFTA. However, education has been assigned a central role in the race of global competitiveness. In May, 1993 a national council on education was announced, to be called the Canadian Forum on Learning, and was to receive seed funding from the federal government.

This federal role in defining education policy reflects a fundamental change for Canada. Education, of course, was assigned to the exclusive responsibility of the provinces in the British North America Act. This was a reflection of the view of education as a central cultural institution that had to reflect the linguistic, religious and cultural choices that differed by province. The provinces have carefully guarded their exclusive territorial claims for education.

In 1975, an external examiner team from the international Organization for Economic Cooperation and Development (OECD) looked at the Canadian education scene and produced a report. The OECD, whose members are pledged to promote economic growth, assists in the co-ordination of the strategies of the major capitalist economies. The OECD examiners noted that unlike other comparable industrialized countries, Canada has not "produced a politically motivated educational reform, rooted in a conception of the country's future.... Instead,

Canada has trodden out its own path ... derived from no explicitly stated, overall national conception of the country's interests."[11]

They also noted significant differences between education in the U.S. and Canada. They said that "many Canadian political and administrative practices can even be regarded as originating in a desire to demonstrate that Canada marches to a different drummer."[12]

The federal Conservative government in the 1980s worked to change both of these facts. It has pushed a politically motivated educational reform based on a transnational corporate conception of the country's interests. And it has tried in many ways, not the least in education, to make sure that Canada marches to the same drummer as in the United States.

This has not been an easy job. Most Canadians opposed the FTA. They opposed cuts to social services. They don't like the shift in taxation from the rich and the corporations to a shrinking middle class. They voted down a proposal to reshape Canada's Constitution. They oppose NAFTA.

A similar story exists in education. The OECD examiners in 1975 concluded that in matters of education policy:

> What may seem to non-Canadians to be 'intolerable' modes of operation are not only tolerated, but accepted happily by most Canadians, because in spite of these modes of operation, they feel (not without justification) that most things to date have gone along quite well.[13] [The parentheses were in the report.]

Undermining Parents' Satisfaction

Parental satisfaction with the schools was still the order of the day in late 1991, according to the federal government itself. As a part of the Prosperity Initiative, a program to restructure a number of Canadian institutions to fit the needs of the transnational corporations, the government issued a 'consultation paper' on education called "Learning Well...Living Well."

Twice in the paper the government acknowledged that it was trying to force a change in education that Canadians don't think they need. In its executive summary, the report states: "By and large, our schools and teachers ably perform the tasks that society assigns to them. The main issue is not what our schools achieve, it is what the Canadian public expects them to achieve."[14]

Further, the report says "Opinion polls confirm that Canadian parents are generally quite satisfied with the educational status quo when it comes to their own children."[15]

'Ignorant' Canadian parents are decried in the "Solution" part of the report: "Public opinion surveys indicate most Canadian parents do not understand that the changing world economy demands a new approach to learning."[16]

Just what is up here, then? Why the great hue and cry from the federal government and the public policy organizations of the corporations?

The answer is pretty clear. Before you can make a reluctant system and public make a change, you must convince them that the current system is failing. What do the corporate leaders want the schools to do that is different from the current system? Again, "Learning Well...Living Well" is more frank about this than the documents produced by the corporate organizations. Less emphasis should be placed on social and cultural elements — those aspects that help to distinguish Canada from the U.S. — and more on economic aspects. It calls for education to be more highly prized for its "impact on individual incomes and national prosperity."[17]

In other words, Canada should be following the 'field of dreams' strategy being pursued by other countries — "build it and they will come." Train your students in the trinity of math, science and technology, and the high-tech jobs will come your way. As the report says, Canada must become "a world leader in math and science achievement at all levels of the school system."[18]

The author of the report also urge an "investments in learning approach." By this they means raising issues of cost/benefit comparisons:

> An investment perspective invites questions about the kind of activities in which we are investing. The schools have done a good job in handling many functions — health, social integration and moral development — that were once felt to be the responsibility of parents, churches and other organizations. But

we should ask if this is a wise way of investing society's resources, does it interfere with the real business of the schools and are there alternative ways of dealing with these problems that would have a better payoff in the long run?[19]

This "better payoff" talk is based on the conventional wisdom spread by these corporate and government reports about just how poorly Canada is doing: reports of dropout rates of 30 per cent and more; reports that Canada comes in at the bottom in international math and science assessments; reports that Canadian children spend less time in school than Japanese children.

The Failure Myth

A careful examination, however, shows that many of the supposed elements of failure of the Canadian education system are in fact mythical. Some examples:

Claim: Canada has a dropout rate of 30 per cent or more.

Reality: A recent Statistics Canada survey indicates that the dropout rate may be as low as 18 per cent. The 30 per cent figure quoted over and over reflected the number of students reported not returning to their school; however, many of the disappeared in fact have registered in other schools, or returned to school after dropping out for a period of time.[20]

Claim: Students in Japan go to school longer than students in Canada.

Reality: A study of the length of time students are in class in Japan and in Canada shows actual class time is about equal. Although Japanese students attend school more days, class time on each of the days they are present is less.[21]

Claim: Not enough Canadian students are taking math.

Reality: In Mathematics, Canada's participation rate was highest of all the countries in the study. In Canada 30 per cent of all youth in the relevant age group are estimated to study Grade 12 Mathematics, as compared to Japan's 12 per cent or England's 6 per cent.[22]

Claim: Not enough Canadian students are taking science.

Reality: With regard to sciences, 'Canadian participation rates were among the highest in all subjects, most notably in chemistry, where the rate is substantially higher than in any other country' (Crocker, 1990, p. 27). For example, English Canada's participation rates were at least one and a half times those of Japan for all three sciences (biology, chemistry and physics)."[23]

Claim: Canadian students score poorly on international science and math tests.

Reality: The figures that show that Canada has high participation also show why average scores would be lower than from school systems that select out only the best students to take these courses. Even where top students are equal, the average score is brought down in the system that has higher participation. The best way to improve Canada's average score is to have fewer students in science and math, but that is not a desirable objective for either the public or corporations.

In other words, a careful look at the claims on which the corporate demands for change are based indicates that not only are they trying to impose American solutions on Canada, they are also trying to define Canada as having the same problems in its education system as does the United States. Certainly there is room for improvement in Canada's schools. But these improvements should be in line with continuing the historical pattern of the schools being increasingly inclusive of more and more students and incorporating social objectives, not just economic objectives.

Under the rubric of 'harmonization', the FTA, NAFTA and the corporate agenda demand that Canada give up some of what it has in order to keep the cost of government competitive in the North American trading bloc.

Harmonization With Poverty

Poverty is a factor that most directly affects children and their ability to participate effectively in school. The FTA-induced deindustrialization of central Canada has been a major factor in the loss of over 435,000 manufacturing jobs, 21.7 per cent of total employment in manufacturing in Canada.[24] This has caused a significant loss of income in many families, a loss accentuated by significant restrictions recently imposed on unemployment insurance passed by the federal Tory government.

Poverty affects school performance in ways ranging from increased violence in the family to loss of concentration because of hunger. At the end of the last decade about 10 per cent of Canadian children lived in poverty compared to about 20 per cent in the United States.[25] But already the downward pressure on social programs is moving those figures closer together.

Another area where Canada's schools are threatened by harmonization pressures is in the financing of education. Canada has been characterized by a high degree of equity in the financing of schools across the country, despite significant inequalities in economic output across the country. The U.S., in contrast, has been characterized by what Kozol has described as "savage inequalities" in a book by that name.

The reasons for this greater equity in Canada are several. One significant factor is the federal revenue equalization, aimed at ensuring that provincial governments have adequate revenues to provide reasonably comparable services at comparable tax rates. This has led to much more equal spending on education from province to province than exists from state to state in our neighbour to the south. In 1990-91, according to Canadian Teachers' Federation (CTF) research, the Canadian province with the lowest level of spending per pupil for elementary and secondary education spent 69.3 per cent of what the highest spending province spent. In contrast, the lowest spending state spent only 32.7 per cent of what the highest state spent.[27]

Inequities are even larger *within* American states, primarily because much of the financing of public education comes from property taxes (49 per cent in the U.S. compared to 27 per cent in Canada).[27] American urban areas have low property values and consequently low ability to produce tax revenues for schools, and high percentages of minority students (e.g., San Francisco — 86 per cent; Boston — 77 per cent; San Antonio — 93 per cent).

In Canada, the federal revenue equalization scheme increases the capacity for the provinces to provide financing from general revenue, and general revenue is generally distributed on the basis of equalization formulas within the province as well.

Canada's medical system also provides more room for public financing of education by working more efficiently. The U.S. spends close to 14 per cent of the gross national product (GNP) on health care, yet 37 million Americans have no health insurance. In contrast, Canada spends less than 10 per cent of its GNP and provides universal coverage. These lower costs in Canada provide more room for public expenditures on education.

Degrading The Teacher Supply

Not surprisingly, Canada has, on an overall basis, better working conditions for teachers and learning conditions for students, and relatively much less inequality.

The CTF reports that "in 1989-90 the national pupil-teacher ratio (PTR) in the United States was 17.2 while that for Canada was 15.9. Interstate variations were over four times greater than interprovincial variations (i.e., the state with the highest PTR — Utah at 25.6 — was nearly double that in the jurisdiction with the lowest PTR — District of Columbia at 13; whereas the province with the highest PTR — Prince Edward Island at 17.3 — was only 17 per cent higher than the province with the lowest PTR — Manitoba at 14.8.)"[28]

Both Canada and the U.S. have historically spent a larger share of national output on education than has Mexico. The average PTR in Mexico in 1987 was 32 at the primary level.

Another area of likely pressure for downward harmonization is in collective bargaining rights. Legislation in Canada is substantially more favourable than that in the U.S. toward the rights of workers to unionize. Less than 16 per cent of the American workforce now belongs to unions, while the rate has stayed around 37 per cent in Canada.

In Canada, all teachers and school support workers in public schools have the right to bargain collectively for their terms and conditions of employment. This has been one of the factors that has helped to maintain both the level of resources devoted to education and to the relative equity that exists across the country.

In contrast, as of the mid-1980s, only 33 U.S. states provided the right for teachers to bargain collectively. In several states only limited bargaining rights exist. In six states laws prohibit collective bargaining and even 'consultation'. So-called 'right-to-work' laws are on the books in 13 states.[29]

One of the reasons cited by the CTF for its opposition to the FTA and now NAFTA is the expected pressure to harmonize labour laws affecting public sector employees in general and teachers in particular. This would undermine "labour law which Canadian teachers depend on in order to bargain collectively for virtually all of their terms and conditions of employment and teaching."[30]

Big Business Moves In

Finally, harmonization will likely create pressure towards more privatization in education, following the trends in the U.S. outlined earlier. Already, imitation of American efforts to bring business into the classroom are widespread.

The Canadian version of Whittle's Channel One, mentioned in Chapter Two, was created by Rod MacDonald, a former organizer for the Conservative party in Manitoba. The Youth News Network (YNN) was to follow the Channel One formula of long-term contracts with schools, with the schools organizing compulsory student viewing in exchange for free video equipment from YNN. The equipment features a computer chip to monitor how often the show is viewed, for how long and at what volume, to make sure the teachers don't 'cheat' and spend the time teaching instead of having the students watch the show.

MacDonald had some initial success in signing on school districts. He hired people who had retired from top administrative positions in school districts to make the pitch for schools to sign up. He even held information meetings for social studies teachers in at least one school district, promising to provide information on how teachers could get free access to teaching materials, but not letting them know that it was going to be a pitch for YNN.

Groups across Canada organized to oppose this attempt to derive commercial gain from student attention. Teacher unions adopted policies opposing YNN. A number of education ministries have expressed opposition to the project.

One district where YNN was seriously considered was in Edmonton. A parent group organized a successful campaign to get the school board to reject YNN. MacDonald struck back with an advertisement in the *Edmonton Journal* warning that "Your teen-ager may be denied an opportunity to participate in YNN because of pressure form some special-interest groups."

YNN has suffered a series of setbacks. The Nova Scotia government rejected an application for a $5 million grant for a studio/production facility in Halifax. YNN was originally scheduled to broadcast in the fall of 1992; it was then postponed to February, 1993, and then had to further delay its premiere.

Less grandiose but increasingly pervasive, U.S.-style business-in-the-school innovations are appearing in Canadian schools as well. For several years a Junior Achievement program called Project Business has brought business people into the Consumer Education program that is compulsory for secondary school students in British Columbia.

In Winnipeg, the U.S. firm Pizza Hut has imported a program — "Book It" — which it sponsors in many American cities. It gives free pizzas as prizes for students who read a specified number of books each month. Of course, students who get the rewards frequently come to the franchise with parents and friends who buy pizzas at the regular price.[31] The program has spread and, according to a recent article in *Canadian Consumer*, in the 1990-91 school year "... close to 250,000 primary school children in 11,000 classrooms took part in Pizza Hut's "Book It" program."[32]

Another U.S. fast-food giant, McDonald's, sponsors a program called "Reading is Fun" for primary school students. The materials "... all prominently feature the golden arches and the McDonald's cast of fun characters."[33]

Many other corporations are now in the business of providing 'educational' materials for primary and secondary schools. EXXON (Imperial Oil) provides brochures on environmental conservation, Procter and Gamble on personal care, and Kelloggs on nutrition.

The Canadian Bankers' Association sponsors a computer game called "Incomes/Outcomes" that gets students to apply economic models to topics like "Who Pays?/Who Gains?: Government's Role in Economic Growth" and "International Trade". The materials are developed and distributed by a group called the Canadian Foundation for Economic Education, which also puts out classroom materials about the free trade deals. The ministries of education in Alberta, Saskatchewan and Manitoba have arranged for distribution of these materials.

While the quality of the corporate material that goes into classrooms varies, all share the same objective: to persuade students that the company's products or its views of an issue are the best of the alternatives. Marketing in schools is even becoming an area of training. "A recent two-day workshop in Toronto, 'Consumer Kids', offered corporate executives such workshops as 'Marketing in the School System' and 'How to Grow Your Customers from Childhood.'"[34]

Another 'innovation' which has recently appeared is the offer of free educational equipment such as computers to schools in return for collecting a specified number of brand labels from food packaging. Students are encouraged to bring in the labels from selected products. Once a sufficient quantity has been collected, their school qualifies for a free computer. This program was introduced by the Grocery Council of Canada and quickly expanded to over 2,000 Ontario elementary schools. When the Vancouver school board refused to approve a similar program, the grocery council took out ads to condemn the board for taking opportunities away from children.[35]

Certainly the easy success of Whittle's Channel One has not been repeated in Canada, and voices are sometimes raised against the other intrusions of corporate marketing into the schools. Although Canadian schools are feeling a squeeze on their funding, they have not yet faced the decades of underfunding that have been the reality in American schools. But the values of commercialism in education will be increasingly difficult to resist in Canada as the pressure for business "partnerships" are entrenched in the national agenda and the harmonization mechanisms of the FTA and NAFTA come into full play.

Chapter Six

NAFTA And Post-Secondary Education In Canada

The FTA and its successor, NAFTA, have seldom been named as the source of major changes in post-secondary education in Canada. But free trade is, increasingly, the driving force behind a fundamental restructuring of Canada's universities, community colleges and other post-secondary institutions. The eventual outcome of this restructuring will be a dramatic increase in the the commercialization and privatization of our post-secondary institutions.

This is not to deny, or minimize, earlier relations between big business and universities. There was a well-documented, if gradual, shift towards a more commercial orientation within academia long before the FTA was negotiated.[1] But, the FTA has given a strong new impetus to the restructuring of post-secondary institutions to accommodate business priorities.[2] NAFTA will further accelerate this process.

How will NAFTA foster much greater corporate involvement in, and influence over, university and community college priorities and decision making? It will do so directly through the new rules which public institutions will have to comply with in their dealings with private companies. But perhaps more importantly, it will do so through unleashing new competitive pressures and a new business culture both in the wider economy and in post-secondary institutions themselves. NAFTA will push governments to make commercial viability the basis for continued funding of educational programs. It will speed up the trend to redirect funding to commercially-oriented programs, while reducing still further the allotments to traditional disciplines, including humanities, arts and social sciences.

Disciplines with little or no obvious commercial value will find it increasingly difficult to justify their funding, while commercially relevant areas — engineering, business administration, the physical sciences, applied mathematics, economics, computer science and the like — will continue to receive funding as long as they carry out research which business sees as important. Universities and other post-secondary institutions will be increasingly pressured to divert resources from the classroom to economically 'relevant' research projects, often in collaboration with corporations.

In addition, NAFTA will unleash new pressures for the international harmonization of post-secondary education along hemispheric lines. Canadian institutions will be drawn into a process of educational integration between Canada, the U.S. and Latin America based on commercial objectives. Their historic academic and cultural ties with Europe and the rest of the world will be weakened, while ever stronger links with Mexico and the rest of the Americas will be forged. This will be carried out not to promote better academic understanding within the hemisphere — a perfectly laudable goal — but rather to satisfy the demands of big business for common standards of training and certification and to satisfy business requirements for an internationally-mobile professional labour force within the free trade area.

If NAFTA is implemented, there will be a plethora of new international partnerships and exchanges among governments, corporations and post-secondary institutions designed to cement Canada's linkages with the U.S. and Latin America. New money will emerge, almost magically, from otherwise hardpressed governments for research and exchanges designed to promote the growing integration of the economies of the hemisphere which the U.S. is anxious to consolidate.

The increasing internationalization of key areas of Canada's post-secondary educational institutions will give the federal government a much greater role in university decision-making. Instead of acting in support of university-initiated activities abroad, the Department of External Affairs, as reshaped by Michael Wilson, will exercise a directive and pro-active role, attempting to shape the kinds of international exchanges in which universities and community colleges participate.

Money will flow freely from the federal government to academics and institutions which put forward initiatives and research projects supportive of the trade agenda. However, for others attempting to fund traditional academic exchanges the well will be dry. Having set in place a process which will eventually terminate its cash contributions to the provinces under the Established Programs Financing (EPF) arrangements, the federal government will be able to target its post-secondary funding directly to projects which it views as being commercially relevant, bypassing provincial governments and forcing universities — and academics — to reshape their priorities or do without.

Many of the changes which are already occurring under free trade are not being advertised as such. The process is incremental and piecemeal, with many of the new arrangements arising out of the broader economic forces unleashed by the trade deal. But change is happening at an accelerating pace. And free trade is at the root of much of this change.

Harmonization: The U.S. Model

The process of hemispheric integration and harmonization fostered by free trade will generate strong pressures for Canadian institutions of higher education to follow the trends which have emerged in the U.S over the past three decades. It is, therefore, important to identify some of the key differences between the Canadian and U.S. systems of higher education and indicate the trends which Canada is likely to end up following under NAFTA.

Canadian universities and colleges have a different history, a different system of funding, different institutions of governance and a different process of accountability to the public than their U.S. counterparts. Certainly, since the rapid expansion of post-secondary education in the 1960s and 1970s, Canadian institutions have been viewed as public institutions accountable to governments (as representatives of the taxpayers) and to the broad educational community. They have not always done this well, but the expectation of public accountability has been there nonetheless.

In the U.S., the most prestigious higher educational institutions are private. Private foundations play a very large role in setting the educational agenda. Grants from the Carnegie, Rockefeller and other foundations have been eagerly sought by universities willing to accept their conditions.[3] Universities have also tended to receive substantial income from military research, a fact which has been the source of controversy since the Vietnam War. And U.S. universities have traditionally raised substantial sums from their alumni.

Historically, U.S. universities have been divided into two groups. The first is composed of the high-status, high-tuition private institutions providing education for a small, relatively wealthy elite. Tuition at these universities is five to 10 times greater than at Canadian universities. Harvard charges $17,470 for an undergraduate arts student, in contrast to $2,026 at the University of Western Ontario. High tuition fees have limited accessibility to all but the brightest and wealthiest students.

The influence and prestige of the private universities has created a 'culture' in which universities address issues of public accountability and public accessibility very differently from universities in Canada. The role of government in directing their affairs has been less significant, while the role of business has been much greater.[4]

Populist Mandate Lost

The second group, the publicly-funded state universities, often started as 'land grant' colleges that were to provide free, or heavily subsidized, higher education for the general population. They were the democratic institutions of higher learning. However, this populist objective was usually restrained by the disproportionate number of appointees to their governing bodies who represented business, professional and commercial interests.

Moreover, the populist mandate of state universities and colleges has been eroded substantially during the postwar period. The emphasis on popular education has been gradually supplanted by commitments to become more 'relevant' to the needs of U.S. industry though a more commercially-oriented curriculum and by diverting more of their resources into corporate research. State universities and colleges have witnessed the emergence of a hierarchy of funding and status, with traditional liberal arts increasingly relegated to the bottom and subjected to ratchet-like fiscal restraint, and the new — and often expanding — business, engineering and science programs at the top, prized because of their commercial relevance.

There has been what David Noble refers to as a "collapse of the distinction between public and private" in the public universities. The 'public' component has largely disappeared, except for the provision of money. They have been largely 'privatized', despite their popular education mandate. Virtually all large U.S. public universities now have satellite research foundations through which public money is channelled to corporate research with virtually no accountability to the taxpayers.

U.S. institutions have also tended to have a much more 'commercial' orientation than have Canadian institutions, reflecting in part the societal commitment to market values and the dominant role of business in many areas of economic and social decision making. There has been less reluctance on the part of U.S. academics to work with large corporations or to enter into money-making arrangements for the commercial exploitation of their research. In turn, U.S. corporations have been eager to establish connections with universities so that they could tap into the expertise of the academic staff and take advantage of the research capacities of well-equipped university labs and other facilities.

U.S. post-secondary education has been more 'commercial' than Canada's in another way. U.S. institutions have a much greater proportion of support services carried out by private firms. This practice of 'contracting out' has been accompanied by the development of very large private service companies who obtain a major portion of their revenues from contracts with post-secondary educational institutions for cleaning, food services, building maintenance, clerical and computing functions and even, in some cases, teaching itself.

The Military Links

U.S. higher education has also had close linkages with the military. Since the beginning of the Cold War, the Pentagon and the defence contractors have made use of the research capabilities of universities to provide them with ideas, technology and innovations. Military research by its very nature tends to be highly secretive. Academics involved in it are constrained to keep their work confidential. Critics have noted that the extensive funding of military research has a profound influence on the academic environment, justifying a highly secretive, centralized decision-making process, undermining public accountability and distorting the priorities of universities.

Although linkages between universities and businesses in the U.S. have existed for generations, a major change began to take place during the mid-1970s.[5] In addition to the traditional relationship where business leaders sat on the boards of governors of universities, university presidents and other senior administrators began to get involved in the corporate world. The creation in 1978 of the Business Higher Education Forum (BHEF) consolidated this development, by bringing together key university presidents and CEOs of major corporations.[6] The organization is divided equally between representatives of each group.

It is now customary for the presidents of major universities — Princeton, Carnegie-Mellon, Chicago and the like — to spend a very large part of their time working as board members of the largest U.S. corporations. According to Noble, these university administrators are being paid hundreds of thousands of dollars annually by the corporations in addition to their university salaries. Their approach to administering the universities they oversee reflects their corporate interests:

> People are using their positions as trustees of public institutions for their private interest, in the name of the public interest. The hijacking of higher education is not an abstraction. It's very

concrete and apparent. It also has names and addresses. And it raises the very serious question of accountability. Who rules the universities and in whose interest?[7]

Moreover, under the influence of the Reagan and Bush administrations U.S. higher education has been pushed into a much closer relationship with business. Universities have been increasingly called upon to help U.S. industry compete more effectively in the global economy. Again, to quote Noble:

> Since 1980, the commercial priorities of academia have become strikingly evident. The thickening web of interlocking directorships between research universities and industry and the proliferation of collaborative university-industry business ties have given the academic leadership a distinctly commercial orientation.[8]

The U.S. post-secondary system has also witnessed another key development: a growing split between well-financed, elite research institutions carrying out corporate and military research and fiscally-starved state universities carrying on traditional liberal arts education. A key player in promoting this distinction has been the American Association of Universities (AAU) which is essentially a cartel of the big research universities, both public and private. The AAU acts as a kind of clearing house and 'match-maker' linking corporations looking for research with universities which have the relevant expertise and facilities.

In sum, U.S. universities have been characterized by their much greater reliance on private funding, their higher tuition, their segregation into elite and mass institutions, their much higher degree of commercialization and their willingness to accept military research as a central component of their financing. While the Canadian system has exhibited some of these characteristics, it is notable for its much greater 'public' character. Historically, there has been less reliance on private finance, much less military research, and a less commercial orientation.

Post-Secondary Profiteering

Other post-secondary training in the U.S. has also been characterized by the large role, and relatively high number, of private institutions. Of the 3.8-million students enrolled in training programs in 1992, 1.6-million or 42 per cent attended private career schools, 396,000 or 10 per cent attended programs sponsored by the Job Training Act and another 55,000 or 1 per cent attended two-year private programs. The total enrolment in public community college programs was 1.46-million or only 38 per cent of all post-secondary places.[9] In comparison with Canada, what is notable is the very large role of private training and the, proportionately, much smaller role for public programs.

The U.S. post-secondary training sector has witnessed the rapid growth in recent years of private, profit-making educational firms, such as Phillips Colleges Inc. which operates 91 subsidiary schools.[10] These chains normally qualify for federal and/or state funding as well as charging tuition to students. They are businesses. And, like businesses, they are run for a profit.

According to the U.S. Department of Education, students attending proprietary schools received over $5.5 billion in public subsidies in 1990 under five major programs.[11]

The encouragement of 'for-profit' training institutions has been seen as responsible for major abuses of public funds, at the expense of students, staff and taxpayers in general.

Phillips, the largest chain, was recently barred from obtaining further federal funds as a result of an audit by the U.S. Department of Education Inspector General. It was cited as having a pattern of "serious and repetitive violations" in its handling of student aid programs.[12] The Inspector General estimated that this decision would result in $225 million of savings to the government. Similar problems were reported in a number of other profit-making schools as a result of the same audit.[13] In the six-month period from April 1, 1992 to September 30, 1992 the Inspector General gave out 82 indictments and had 97 convictions for misapplication of public funds by private schools.[14]

The point is not that abuses exist, but rather that the system of public funding has been structured to provide profit-making opportunities for large numbers of private training companies. Money which in Canada — at least until recently — would go to community colleges, is channelled in the U.S. to private institutions. Moreover, private training in this sector has grown dramatically in the U.S. since the early 1970s, particularly under Reagan and Bush.[15]

The trend towards a post-secondary education system totally subordinated to business objectives might not be of much interest to Canadians if there were adequate mechanisms to prevent any 'spillover' of these developments to Canada. However, the reality of closer economic integration with the U.S. means that this trend points to the future of our institutions as well.

This is not to deny that Canadian universities were moving closer to the corporate world in the decade before Canada passed the FTA. But it is to recognize that the ethos in Canada before the FTA was still strongly public. Commercial priorities were important, but not all-pervasive. Since the deal was put in place, there has been a virtual sea change in the policy direction of universities, colleges and other post-secondary institutions. We are witnessing a massive privatization and commercialization of our public institutions.

Canada's Public Approach

Historically, the Canadian government has not had primary constitutional responsibility for education. This is the prerogative of the provinces. In the early postwar period, under the Liberals, the federal government gradually became more and more involved in post-secondary education. It wanted to promote the expansion of Canada's university system and was prepared to offer money to the provinces to achieve this objective.

Consequently, it negotiated new funding programs with the provinces. Initially these were based on a 50-50, cost-sharing formula. Largely as a result of this infusion of federal money, the university system expanded dramatically during the 1960s and early 1970s.

What is notable about the rapid growth of the federal government's involvement in post-secondary education during the 1950s, 1960s and early 1970s is that it was designed to build and strengthen Canada's public university system. The new federal interest in this area paralleled other initiatives it took during the same period including hospital insurance, medicare and the Canada Assistance Plan. The assumption was that a basic right of citizenship was access to the same social programs, regardless of province of residence or the fiscal capacity of that province. The expansion of public programs was desirable and appropriate in the context of a mixed economy in which there was a 'balance' between public and private sectors.

Accessibility and affordability were also key goals of the Canadian system. Tuition fees provided only a small proportion of the total cost of a university student's education. Federal and provincial governments picked up the remainder. Canadian public policy towards education was designed to minimize financial barriers to students.

The Crackdown Begins

However, in the mid-1970s the federal government began to rein in its expenditures.[16] Its concern about uncontrolled inflation, its worry about its own fiscal problems, its belief that it was not getting adequate credit for funding national programs and its view that the cost-sharing system provided an incentive for provinces to spend ever greater sums of money on public programs — because the more they spent the more federal money they got — led to a decision to place a cap on federal contributions. The federal government accordingly pushed the provinces into replacing the 50-50, cost-sharing formula with a combination of tax points and cash transfers.[17]

The provinces accepted this because they were permitted to redirect money raised from tax points to other budgetary priorities. The federal government, in turn, got a cap on the funding it was committed to give provinces for post-secondary education. Federal cash transfers were calculated on the basis of a complex formula which took into account growth in population, GDP (Gross Domestic Product), inflation and various regional factors. This new system was consolidated in the Established Programs Financing Act in 1977.

From the late 1970s until the election of the Tories in 1984, the Liberals carried out a number of cost-cutting measures through amendments to the transfer formula. However, the basic assumption remained that public funding for post-secondary education would grow in parallel with the overall growth in the economy and the increase in population. Moreover, the system was still viewed as overwhelmingly a 'public' system in which commercial concerns co-existed with a range of other more traditional academic and pedagogical objectives.

The Tories Take Over

The attitude of the newly-elected Mulroney government was very different. The Tories unilaterally reduced the EPF funding formula (without provincial agreement). Legislation reducing federal funding was introduced in 1985 and again in 1989. In 1990, the Tories passed Bill C-69. This bill froze federal cash transfers to the provinces through EPF until 1992. It then capped the rate of growth for 1993 and subsequent years to the GNP minus 3 per cent. The following year, Bill C-20 was passed. It extended the freeze for an additional two years, accelerating the federal government's withdrawal from EPF education funding for the provinces. According to the Canadian Association of University Teachers (CAUT), between 1990-91 and 1995-96 the provinces will lose a total of $4.4 billion as a result of these cuts. Starting with Quebec in the late 1990s, federal cash transfers will end for all provinces shortly after the turn of the century.

This policy of withdrawing federal money signifies a major retreat from the principle of providing a national system of properly-financed, accessible and affordable public universities. A process of slow strangulation was set in motion, precipitating continual cuts in staffing, sharp increases in tuition, crumbling physical infrastructure, loss of support services and a general deterioration in the quality of education available to students who are enrolled in the traditional liberal arts areas.

At the same time, the public money still coming into the system is being redirected to disciplines with commercial relevance. The historic 'balance' among humanities, liberal arts, sciences and the professions has been tilted dramatically towards business-based education and research. On almost every campus, the decline of funding for liberal arts is paralleled by growth and new construction of management schools, engineering facilities, medical research laboratories and other practical, commercially-viable research areas. In the words of

Claire Polster:

Since 1987, for example, cuts in federal transfer payments to the provinces for post-secondary education have cost Canadian universities something in the neighbourhood of $2.4 billion. At the same time that this sizeable amount of money has been taken out of the base operations of the universities, a lot of money has been reinjected into the higher-education system through a variety of government programs and initiatives, the most celebrated of which is InnovAction, the $1.3 billion federal science and technology strategy.[18]

The federal money the Tories are still putting into higher education is increasingly being tied to specific research areas with commercial spin-offs.

Money which once went to liberal arts through EPF is now allocated through federal granting agencies such as the Natural Sciences and Engineering Research Council (NSERC) and to programs such as the Centres of Excellence, which bring together university researchers and corporations to work on practical applications of scientific and technical work done on elite campuses. The federal government has also reallocated training money formerly spent on community college programs to new private training schemes.

In short, the traditional 'core' of the public system — liberal arts — is being deliberately cut back while a number of major new private sector initiatives are being promoted. Public education is being jettisoned to facilitate commercial objectives.

Free Trade And Commercialization

Although the tendency was evident before 1989, free trade accelerated the move towards the commercialization of educational institutions and the privatization of educational services. These developments are deeply intertwined. Public institutions are being reshaped according to commercial values and commercial objectives. At the same time many of their functions are being transferred to the private sector. Both these issues merit further examination.

What is commercialization? In its broadest terms, it means the application of commercial criteria to the assessment of the worth of academic and educational programs. Commercialization has a number of overlapping features.[19]

One is the rapid adoption of the principles and values of business management by the administrators of post-secondary institutions.

It shows in the language they use. The concepts and language of business management have quickly taken over as the operating *modus vivendi* of the new breed of university presidents and senior administrative staff. Faculty are paid employees. Education is a 'product' which managers 'market'. Students are 'consumers' and corporations are 'stakeholders'. In short, campuses are now dominated by a new breed of 'corporate' managers whose objectives are to run the institution internally, like a business, while promoting its services externally, like a company selling a product. And the 'product' is no longer solely education for students; it is commercially relevant research.

As public funding is being choked off, marketing becomes a big thing. A university has to sell itself to generate enough revenue to flourish in hard times. The result is that programs, and even entire departments, are assessed on whether they can meet the test of commercial viability or, minimally, commercial relevance.[20] New programs are established not fundamentally for academic reasons, but because they will enable the university to tap into public or private research money. Existing programs are restructured so that they can attract potential revenue. Or, they are closed down.[21]

The new university managers have also adopted a lifestyle which increasingly resembles that of the corporate executives they pattern themselves on and interact with on a regular basis. And this is occurring in the context of rapid tuition increases, cuts in staffing, deteriorating classrooms and physical plant and the strangulation of funding for more traditional academic activities.[22] While more and more teaching is done by grossly underpaid sessionals, the number of senior administrators grows steadily in relation to tenured faculty in the university.[23]

The managerial approach has also encouraged senior administrators to treat the public institutions they administer as if they were their own private property. Wheeling and dealing, they adopt policies which enable them to use university resources to support their pet projects and commercial activities. They award themselves expenses and perks (e.g., interest free loans, free housing, travel and other benefits) which parallel those received by senior business executives. Simultaneously, they reject calls for greater public accountability or for the increased participation of other members of the university community in decision making. Increasingly, they make the claim that universities are really 'private' institutions which are not required to account for their activities to the public.

Commercialization has not been limited to the senior administrators of universities and community colleges. Individual faculty members in many disciplines now see themselves as 'academic entrepreneurs'.[24] They set up their own companies, hire research assistants to work on their corporate projects and make deals with businesses and the university concerning a wide range of commercial matters. Making profit is now seen not only as acceptable, but as a desirable activity in many departments — a sign of business savvy and 'making it' in the real world. Indeed, it is fair to say that there is a growing group of faculty who are now basically business persons who happen to hold tenured jobs at universities, jobs which provide the base and connections to get on with their real work: making money. According to Polster, the federal government is actively encouraging this process:

> In addition to promoting these 'entrepreneurial academics', the governments are also facilitating their creation. Through a variety of structures and services that have been rapidly expanding over the last 15 years (such as offices of technology transfer) government is helping to provide academics with the necessary advice and resources to help them market, patent, and/or licence the results of their own research.[25]

The faculty, as entrepreneurs, are not, of course, the dominant players in this scenario. The corporations are. They are given access to university resources and staff at little or no cost. They are able to piggy-back their need for research onto the publicly-funded research projects of the faculty. And, frequently, they are able to benefit from the patents and copyrights resulting from publicly-funded research. These developments have been summarized concisely in a recent article by John Harris:

> In their search for cash, universities are opening their doors to business. Knowledge that was free, open and for the benefit of society is now proprietary, confidential and for the benefit of private companies. Educators who once jealously guarded their autonomy now negotiate curriculum planning with corporate sponsors. Senior faculty put aside troubling ethical considerations for a shot at the first-class travel, generous per diem expense accounts and whopping salary increases that accompany university participation in questionable, but profitable Third-World development projects. Professors who once taught are now on company payrolls churning out marketable research in the campus lab, while universities pay cut-rate fees for replacement teaching assistants to churn out students in auditorium-sized classrooms. University presidents, once the intellectual leaders of their institutions, are now accomplished bagmen, with some spending more than half their time on the road making deals for cash.[26]

Of course, not every discipline is commercially relevant. Academics teaching traditional subjects such as classics, English, history and the like are far less likely to get ahead as entrepreneurs when compared with their colleagues in business administration, engineering, medicine and the hard sciences. Universities are thus becoming more and more divided between faculty who are deeply involved in commercial activities and those who are unable to get on this new gravy train. In the words of Donald Savage, former president of the CAUT:

> The business community isn't interested in the humanities or social sciences and wants to put its money into the largest institutions.[28]

This division between commercially relevant and non-commercial research also undermines opposition to the commercialization of the universities, as many academics have developed a vested interest in the new approach to university functions. It also creates a new hierarchy of income, status and research opportunities, as the new academic entrepreneurs are able to acquire a greater and greater share of public and private funding — funding which is increasingly being targeted specifically at projects which will make Canada more 'competitive'.

Funding Tied To Commercialization

Commercialization has also been fostered by new approaches to funding post-secondary education by provincial and federal governments. Increasingly, funding — particularly at the community college level — is being allocated not on the basis of enrolment, but on the basis of 'competition' among institutions. As John Huot of Humber College in Toronto notes:

> Colleges now have to compete in the market for government and corporate training funding, frequently by tender to the specific requirements of employers. They compete not just with other colleges and public educational institutions, but also with profit-based and non-profit-based organizations. With revenues from government sources declining, colleges are encouraged to aggressively pursue market-driven opportunities to remain financially viable. For many colleges, this new source of revenues is the strategic priority in their long term planning.[28]

The federal government ties its financial assistance to business objectives by putting more money directly into the hands of faculty members carrying out commercially relevant research as it slashes its EPF cash transfers to the province. By 1991, individual grants amounted to over $160 million annually. This approach enables the federal government to reshape the research agendas of universities without having to fight with the provinces over the priorities it is promoting.[29]

The federal government has also moved to change the mandate of federal-funding agencies such as NSERC. Its purpose is to "... provide opportunities to exploit the special knowledge and expertise at Canadian universities for the benefit of industry and the Canadian Economy."[30] The tens of millions of dollars annually given out by this agency are now being directed into research which conforms to this mandate.

The Centres Of Excellence Program

In 1988, the Tory government unveiled a new program to link universities and corporations together through a high-tech, computerized research network. Referred to somewhat pretentiously as the Networks of Centres of Excellence, the program was the centrepiece of the $1.3-billion federal government InnovAction initiative. It was given a $245-million budget over five years. By 1993, 15 universities and 800 researchers were linked with over 170 companies in joint research projects.[31]

According to one of its strongest supporters, Arthur May, president of Memorial University, the purpose of the new network is:

> ... helping to lay the foundation of a new economy — one that is knowledge-based and high-tech. It is speeding up our ability to climb out of the old smokestack-filled, recession-plagued economy and compete with our G-7 trading partners in such growth areas as biotechnology, pharmaceutical, telecommunications and semi-conductors.[32]

May notes a wide range of research which is now being carried out in these sectors. There is an Ocean Production Enhancement Network for fisheries research in which National Sea Products plays a key role. There is a High Performance Concrete Network which is working with the cement companies to find new ways to mould concrete. There are networks looking into enzymes, pulp and paper processes, genetic screening and microelectronics, to cite some of the other key areas. The program also encourages young graduates and scientists "... to take into account the economic applicability of their research."[33]

However, one of the major criticisms of the federally-funded centres is that the money has been allocated primarily to very large research 'mega' projects, involving $10 million to $20 million each. These mega-projects may well fit in with the goals of the larger corporations who wish to benefit from the research, but they provide little support for the work of thousands of other researchers who do not require anything like the investment associated with these projects and whose work may be academically valuable, if not commercially marketable.[34] In targeting such mega-projects, the federal government is effectively ensuring that the corporations will get the research they need and in a form which is readily manageable.

The Space University Proposal

There has also been the first — but undoubtedly not the last — attempt to establish a new private university, explicitly intended to provide research to large multinational corporations. This occurred at the campus of York University, where a proposal was widely promoted to establish a new International Space University (ISU) on campus.[35]

The ISU Project, Inc. has existed since 1987 on a temporary campus at the Massachusetts Institute of Technology with support from NASA and a number of U.S. military contractors. The proponents of ISU planned to find a permanent campus through a process of advertising and soliciting bids from the U.S. and other countries.

York University's bid was supported by the newly-elected Ontario NDP government which saw the hosting of this high-tech campus as a way to promote research and development within the province.

However, closer scrutiny of the ISU proposal revealed some very disturbing information. Although it was supposed to be promoting non-military space research, almost all the U.S. donations it received, totalling $285,000 between 1987 and 1990, were from major defence contractors, including Rockwell, McDonnell Douglas, Boeing, Lockheed and TRW. NASA contributed another $333,000 during the same period in start-up funding. Canadian private sector support for the York bid also came from major military suppliers.[36]

Private corporations were to be accorded special research rights. Even more significant was the plan to establish ISU as a private university — a fundamental break with Ontario's tradition of public universities. Nevertheless, this 'private' university campus would have special access to the facilities of York University including representation on the Senate and the right to give York degrees. Neither the students, faculty, members of the Senate or the campus unions were told of these special arrangements. Tuition levels were also projected to be $25,000 per year for the 200 graduate students it would host. Finally, the faculty to be employed by ISU would not be governed by the normal hiring and immigration requirements.[37]

Once the details of the ISU proposal leaked out to the public, there was a groundswell of opposition. Although the deal was virtually 'done', the sponsors of the ISU had a last-minute change of heart. On the morning of the final announcement there was a champagne breakfast organized by its supporters to celebrate York's acquisition of the centre. To their dismay, the decision awarded the ISU to Strasbourg, France. The protests in Canada had succeeded in blocking it. The university climate in Canada was apparently not considered suitably stable — it was populated by too many crazy Canadian protesters — for the project to go to Toronto.

The ISU was intended to introduce the U.S. approach of providing public support for private universities. It followed the U.S. practice of elite tuition requirements. It formally introduced the U.S. practice of incorporating research with military applications as a legitimate part of the university's mandate. And, it formalized the U.S. practice of defining the university mandate as quite explicitly one of being a vehicle for corporate research. Of course, there have been elements of all these developments in existence at Canadian universities in the past. But ISU attempted to push this agenda much further, setting new precedents for the future. The ISU is a precursor of new hemispheric partnerships between governments, universities and business.

University Officials And Corporate Directors

Historically, many university boards of governors have been populated by business people. Being a member of a university board has long been a status symbol. Academics and administrators have also used their university positions to open doors in the business world, in some cases enabling them to take new jobs as corporate executives.

But in the commercialization of universities, the roles of university administrators and faculty have changed. The emergence of the administrator (or academic) as business entrepreneur has caused unease in some circles about the potential for conflict of interest between the public trust placed in these people and their increasing ability to use their public positions for commercial interests.

In the autumn of 1992, the Senate of the University of British Columbia (UBC) debated a new set of guidelines for university administrators holding corporate directorships. The debate focused on an amendment proposed by political science professor Philip Resnick that would have required deans and administrators sitting on corporate boards to donate any remuneration to the university.

The University Senate rejected Resnick's amendment and passed the main proposal which required that all faculty, deans and administrators obtain approval from the university before accepting directorships. They could, however, keep any payments received. The new rules also apply to directorships in advocacy and non-profit organizations.

According to the *Vancouver Sun*, Resnick said that he wanted the university to avoid "… set(ting) itself up for the accusation it was in the pocket of private paymasters."[38]

One reason the issue provoked heated debate is that a number of senior administrators at UBC were already deeply involved in corporate activities. UBC president David Strangway was on the boards of MacMillan Bloedel, B.C. Gas, Royal Trust, the Japan Society of Canada, the International Institute for Sustainable Development and Echo Bay Mining.[39] The Dean of Forestry, Clark Binkley, who holds a directorship in West Fraser Timber Co. Ltd., was also a board member of Eco-Trust, an ecology association. According to the *Vancouver Sun*, "other UBC deans and administrators serve on different corporate boards. Many professors also have direct links to private companies."[40]

Resnick also claimed that government cutbacks, coupled with increased corporate funding for research and development, was channelling universities into projects focusing on short-term business goals, rather than more traditional academic scholarship.

Canadian universities have also begun to copy the U.S. pattern of establishing foundations and trusts and other corporate entities as a way of making deals with the business sector. One example of this is the University of Toronto Innovations Foundation. It is described in its promotional literature as a "Technology Licensing Company Founded by the University of Toronto." According to its advertising, "its mission is to select, protect (patent), market and licence commercially promising technologies which result from research conducted at the University of Toronto, its affiliated institutions, centres of excellence and other universities or corporations."[41]

Many universities now have an office of 'intellectual property' with full-time staff who specialize in connecting patentable research with commercial firms. These spin-off foundations provide a way for universities to engage in a wide range of contractual business relationships without having to fully disclose the nature of the deals they sign. Under the guise of protecting proprietary knowledge or maintaining commercial secrecy, public accountability is restricted or denied.

Universities As Corporate Advocates

The establishment of close commercial ties between universities and corporations has also made some universities into virtual advocacy organizations for corporate interests. Increasingly, companies are enlisting the aid of their university partners in campaigns to change legislation or obtain special tax or other benefits from governments. Because universities are widely perceived as disinterested, neutral and objective in their assessment of public policy issues, their support of business is particularly effective.

Alliances with business, however, are apt to make universities more concerned about the private interests they are in bed with than the broader public interest they are widely seen to represent. Perhaps the most notable example of this new trend is the support given by a number of universities to Bill C-91, which extended the length of exclusivity for drug patents to 20 years.

In October, 1992, the Coalition for Biomedical and Health Research was founded. The purpose of this organization was to generate public support for additional funding for drug-related research. According to a recent article in the *Toronto Star* by David Noble and Maude Barlow, this organization brought together the Association of Canadian Medical Colleges, representing 16 university faculties of medicine; the Canadian Federation of Biological Societies with a membership of 17 scientific organizations and over 6,000 biological and biomedical scientists; and the Health Research Foundation of the Pharmaceutical Manufacturers' Association.[42] The latter organization represents the foreign-controlled pharmaceutical companies.

Bill C-91 is directly connected to the Intellectual Property chapter of NAFTA. It had to be passed by Parliament for Canada to meet the new requirements of the trade deal. In contrast to 1988, when the federal government disingenuously took the position that the extension of drug patents was not connected with free trade, the more far-reaching 1992 legislation was clearly acknowledged to be a precondition of the implementation of NAFTA.

The effect of Bill C-91 is to enable the foreign-controlled pharmaceutical manufacturers to raise the prices of patented drugs and keep them up without having to worry about competition from Canadian-made 'generic' equivalents for 20 years. The estimated costs of this extension of patent protection to the Canadian public are going to be very substantial — up to $4 billion, according to one source.[49]

The first major public activity of the newly-founded Coalition for Biomedical and Health Research was to lobby the federal government to pass Bill C-91 as quickly as possible. The dean of medical research at Dalhousie University, who serves as chair of the Coalition, was a very active supporter of the legislation on the grounds that his university was promised $1.5 million annually for five years by the world's largest drug company, Merck Frosst, if the legislation were enacted. He is quoted by Barlow and Noble, who reported:

> 'I realize that in relative terms, this ($1.5 million annually) represents a small amount if it can in fact buy our support for Bill C-91', Dickson acknowledged, but he expressed his 'hope' that this scientific sell-out would prove more fruitful for biomedical research in the long run.[44]

Dalhousie was not the only university co-opted to support the position of the foreign drug companies. At about the same time, UBC announced that it had worked out a research and development deal with Merck Frosst. While the precise terms of the deal remain private, what has been revealed is that the firm offered to invest a total of $15 million for a genetics research centre at UBC in return for the university's support of the controversial drug patent bill.[45]

One of the most disturbing aspects of this issue was the willingness of senior university officials to campaign in support of the company's position. They became deeply embroiled in a major public debate around health care policy because they were concerned that Merck Frosst would abandon its research commitment if it did not get the changes to patent legislation. The fact that a number of influential researchers had become dependent on corporate grants was clearly a factor in the university's position.

But the consequence of their desire to maintain corporate funding for their projects was to mobilize the prestige and status of a public institution — UBC — in support of the private interests of the world's largest drug company. Many critics saw the university's actions as a betrayal of the larger public interest, as well as the specific interests of the Canadian generic drug industry and Canadian drug consumers.

The irony of this position is that most of the research money spent in university laboratories is still public money. Large multinational corporations are able to acquire the fruits of taxpayer-funded research by obtaining exclusive control of the resulting patents and copyrights. They are then able to turn around and charge taxpayers monopoly prices — prices based on exclusive control of these patents — for the very same research the public has already paid for. As Barlow and Noble note:

> Thus Industry investment in academic research actually turns out to be more of a subsidy to industry than the other way around, a privatization of the benefits, through patent and licensing arrangements, but not the costs. Thus the public continues to underwrite the bulk of the research, yet forfeits control over the results.[46]

It is perhaps unfair to highlight York, UBC and Dalhousie for their particular business activities. Many other universities across Canada have been energetically building corporate alliances. The University of Waterloo houses some of the oldest business-university research partnerships. Under the leadership of recently retired president Doug Wright, Waterloo has become perhaps the leading university in doing deals with business.

Literally hundreds of other business-university partnerships can be documented at campuses across Canada. Some of these partnerships date back as far as the 1960s, or earlier. But since the mid-1980s they have increased dramatically. Also notable is the much more assertive, self-confident approach which business and universities are now taking towards these partnerships. Whereas several decades ago the propriety of universities making commercial arrangements was seen as debatable, it is now taken for granted by many that universities should be pushing to build commercial ties.

Formalizing The Linkages

In 1983, a new organization, the Corporate-Higher Education Forum (C-HEF), was founded. It brought together the presidents of 32 Canadian universities with the chief executive officers of 38 major corporations. These include companies such as Bell Canada, Imperial Oil, Xerox, Quaker Oats, Lafarge, Bombardier, Spar Aerospace, Hewlett Packard, Bank of Montreal, Loblaws, IBM, Dow, Laidlaw, Shell, London Life, Dofasco, Alcan, Du Pont, General Electric, Canadian Pacific and many other major firms.

Modelled on the BHEF in the U.S., the C-HEF has worked to promote partnerships between business and universities in a wide range of areas. At the same time, it has lobbied for continued fiscal restraint by governments on the grounds that business should play a much greater role in university financing. It has also pushed for market principles in the operation of university programs.[47]

Since its foundation, the C-HEF has published a number of major policy statements and hosted an annual conference bringing together senior executives and university administrators.[48] Among its publications is a guide to writing contracts between business and universities. The guide, entitled "Spending Smarter (Update)", was put together by Donald P. Assaf, director of university liaison for Bell Canada.

The guide provides universities and companies with a number of options regarding issues such as confidentiality and the ownership and exploitation of intellectual property. On the ownership of intellectual property, the C-HEF provides a number of approaches, but these are clearly biased towards enabling corporations to maximize the benefits the acquire from shared research projects. In their words:

The question of who has the right to so called "Intellectual Property" in a research endeavour is a very complex one. In the first place, the particular project may be a portion of a large body of knowledge which resides in the university or in the corporation or both. It is obviously important for both the corporation and the university to limit disclosure to the project at hand. One should also anticipate that the work may trigger ideas or open up paths of investigation for the researchers. Instead of trying to capture some of these rather ephemeral aspects of the transaction, *Option 1* is structured in such a way that the "Deliverables" and other Intellectual Property, belong to the company.[49]

The actual text of the recommended agreement provides that "the deliverables specified in Article 3 and any other intellectual property described above shall be owned by the Company, including assignment of any rights to inventions."[50]

The C-HEF has acted as the chief spokesperson of big business in the area of education. Its counterpart on economic and social policy issues — the BCNI — has generally allowed the C-HEF to take the lead in advocating changes to Canada's educational programs.

While the BCNI tends to allow the Forum to take the lead in educational policy issues, in a rather awkwardly named working paper, "Building a New Century Economy: The Canadian Challenge", the BCNI sets out a very brief agenda for restructuring education. According to this document, Canada has:

> ... over-invested in 'generalized' post-secondary education through an extensive network of colleges and universities that largely duplicate their programs. At the same time, we have under-invested in more specialized research programs, as well as in technical and vocational training that is closely linked to specific careers.[51]

The voice of big business wants more of the public money currently spent on education to be allocated to specialized, elite institutions which can better carry out high-quality research in conjunction with the private sector. It also wants federal money to be targeted primarily to research through the research granting councils and the centres of excellence program.

To pay for this shift, it suggests that general, non-specialist educational programs be trimmed back or eliminated. And, it argues that students should be required to pay substantially higher tuition: "The proportion of post-secondary costs covered from tuition income should rise gradually from today's 20 per cent to closer to 35 per cent."[52]

The BCNI also wants the federal government to replace the current system of transfers to the provinces under EPF with a system which would allocate the money directly to students. Students would be free to purchase educational services from whichever institution — public or private — they preferred. More importantly, by channelling student grants into particular areas, the federal government could redefine the priorities of the universities without having to become directly involved in their governance.

Finally, the BCNI gives a higher priority to fiscal restraint by governments than to increasing public funding to post-secondary education. It acknowledges the fact that "... quality is deteriorating and parts of the universities' research infrastructure are in peril...." But it argues that, in light of the deficits faced by governments, "... it is unrealistic to expect them to increase their financial support to post-secondary education in any significant way."[53]

If implemented, the changes proposed by the BCNI would bring us much closer to the U.S. approach to post-secondary education. The system would be significantly more commercial in its orientation. The private sector would play a much greater role. Tuition would be increased towards U.S. levels. And, public funds would be shifted to provide much greater support for the research and development needs of business.[54]

The Hemispheric Harmonization

Re-orienting Canada's approach to international education has also been a key element of the Tory government's agenda for selling NAFTA.

This is part of a broader Tory strategy to redirect Canada's commercial, trade and foreign policy activities and mesh them with its new hemispheric approach to economic development. This change has been so marked that even the *Globe and Mail's* European bureau chief, Madelaine Drohan, commented on it in a recent feature article:

> Canadian foreign policy has done and about-face since the heady days of Louis St. Laurent and Lester B. Pearson, when Canada saw itself as an international player with interests beyond North America. Politically, commercially and militarily, it is drawing back into its continental shell, severing links that had been painstakingly forged since the Second World War. Diplomatic posts are being cut, development and aid programs scaled down and the national focus redirected south to the United States and beyond....
>
> Canada ... has chosen the first option, binding itself to the U.S. through the Canada-U.S. Free Trade Agreement and the North American free trade accord. It's a choice that Rainer-Olaf Schultz, a German academic who heads the Institute for Canadian Studies at Augsburg University in Germany, says will lead to political and monetary union with the U.S. 'Contrary to what the Canadian politicians are saying, that's the next step.'[55]

Yet, while Canada is closing consulates and embassies in Europe, Africa and Asia, the Department of External Affairs has spent (and will spend) tens of millions of new dollars promoting business-to-business exchanges between Canada and Mexico as part of the government's effort to build a stronger business constituency in support of NAFTA, and to get Canadian businesses to invest in Mexico.

But the academic world has not been overlooked. Indeed, a significant part of the free trade agenda is to get Canadian universities to support the trade and investment activities of Canadian businesses within the new hemispheric market.

This approach is a break with Canada's past. Formerly, academics and education policy-makers looked primarily to the U.S. and to Europe (and in B.C. to Japan and the Far East), rather than to Latin America for opportunities to exchange ideas and foster international co-operation. However, just as the Tories have abandoned the previous Liberal government's 'third option' (i.e., greater trade with Europe) for Canadian economic development in favour of integration with the U.S., they have also sought to redirect the focus of international educational exchanges to conform to the new hemispheric market established by the trade deal.

In itself, expanding educational exchanges with Latin America is desirable and perhaps long overdue, given Canada's geography. But the purpose with NAFTA is not to encourage the traditional kinds of international academic exchanges. The point is to foster a particular, business-oriented process which will focus Canadian educational initiatives on providing support for Canadian corporations expanding into Latin America.

Going Commercial

A key element cementing the trade deal is a new approach to international educational exchanges. This approach is intended to foster hemispheric co-operation in developing common standards of education, training and labour mobility. Through this process — which at one level can be described simply as a long-overdue attempt to recognize the reality of Canada's geography and to redress Canada's narrow and isolationist approach to Latin America — Canada will gradually be drawn in to the new economic and political framework which former U.S. President Bush referred to as the "Enterprise of the Americas" initiative.

The purpose of greater international co-operation is not simply, or primarily, to promote educational objectives. Rather, it is to reshape education throughout the hemisphere to conform to the commercial, investment and labour force development requirements of transnational corporations. Traditional educational objectives in all three countries will be supplanted by narrow, economic concerns to the detriment of national cultural traditions.

Not surprisingly, since the possibility of NAFTA was first voiced there has been a flurry of meetings, conferences, exchanges and academic papers addressing the issue of hemispheric co-operation. These initiatives have been pushed along by the three governments who are anxious to establish as many linkages as possible among educational administrators and academics so that they can be brought on board the tri-national economic agreement.

In September, 1992, a tri-national education conference was held at the Wingspread Conference Centre in Racine, Wisconsin entitled "North American Higher Education: Identifying the Agenda." The Wingspread conference brought together senior educational officials and university administrators from the three countries to discuss how to promote co-operation and international exchanges.[56]

Among those listed in attendance were Alain Dudoit, director general of the International Cultural Relations Bureau of the Canadian Department of External Affairs; James Fox, president of the Canadian Bureau for International Education; Claude Hamel, president of the Université du Québec; Shell Harvey, assistant deputy minister, of the B.C. Ministry of Advanced Education, Training and Technology; Donald Johnston, principal of McGill University; David Strangway, president of UBC; Robert Prichard, president of the University of Toronto; Doug Wright, president of the University of Waterloo; John Mallea, former president of Brandon University; Tom Norton, president of the Association of Canadian Community Colleges; Louise Dandurand, executive director of the Social Sciences and Humanities Research Council of Canada; and, George Molloy, director of research and development for the Council of Ministers of Education.[57]

What is notable about the list of participants is that other members of Canada's educational community were left out. Nobody from teacher organizations, faculty associations or labour unions appear to have been invited. The process was restricted to a small elite of educational policy-makers.

The delegations from the U.S. and Mexico were equally high-powered, including key officials from the respective ministries of education and key academic administrators from prestigious universities. The same elite bias is evident in their delegations.

The conference participants endorsed a joint statement which they recommended for consideration by the educational authorities and decision-makers in each country. The statement reads as follows:

1. Internationalization of higher education in our three countries is the key to improvement of the quality of education and research; the standard of living of the citizens of our countries and the overall quality of life within our respective countries; and better understanding of our respective distinctive cultures and identities.

2. Better understanding and acceptance of our distinctive realities are essential components of stronger partnerships, greater access to the vast North American potential, and effective development of our countries' growing relationships.
3. Enhanced trilateral collaboration in higher education builds upon existing relationships and benefits our three countries. This statement is made with full recognition of and respect for the national sovereignty of our respective countries, the responsibilities of our different jurisdictions, and the autonomy of our higher education institutions.
4. Enhanced trilateral higher education collaboration provides additional impetus to greater co-operation within our respective countries and supports bilateral relations with third countries and relevant multilateral organizations.

The participants also outlined a six-point program of practical initiatives. These included a request to the three governments to interpret the services chapter of NAFTA in a manner which would permit academics, university administrators and students to be included in the special professional immigration category. (This would facilitate trilateral exchanges.)

This conference was followed by another in Guadalajara, Mexico "... which took a critical look at the characteristics of North American academic co-operation and the role of universities, associations, and private foundations in expanding free trade."[58] A further conference to follow up on the Wingspread meeting is being planned for the UBC during September, 1993.

The merits of developing better ties among the three countries are clear, but the real issue is on what basis these new linkages will be established. Will they be commercial or will they be based on more traditional academic values and objectives? While many of the academics and educators may honestly desire the latter, the underlying purpose of the governments is to provide further support to the trade deal itself.

Indeed, several prominent U.S. educators including Alan Adelman and Patricia Somers are already calling for the creation of an "Academic Common Market in North America."[59] The U.S. and Mexico have already set up a 'debt for development' program which will enable U.S. universities to buy Mexican debt, in the form of pesos at a discount (currently 20 per cent) and use the money to fund educational programs they would establish in Mexico.[60]

In late 1992, Canada, the U.S. and Mexico agreed to establish a high-powered "Trilateral Task Force on North American Higher Education." Part of the work of this task force will be to plan the conference at UBC in September, 1993. According to a U.S. Information Agency press release,[61] Canadian involvement in this process is being co-ordinated by Dudoit of the Department of External Affairs. He is also the official Canadian representative on the three-person steering committee.

The central role of this department in the exchanges which are now being encouraged underlines the close connection with the free trade deal which the same department helped negotiate. It also raises serious questions about the extent to which Canada's international educational exchanges are being subordinated to the trade and investment priorities of the Department of External Affairs, rather than the traditional academic interest in the international sharing of knowledge.

Lament For The Arts

In the preceding pages we have documented the trend towards commercializing and privatizing Canada's post-secondary educational institutions. These developments fall in line with the U.S. model. Although many of the changes we are now witnessing were becoming apparent before the free trade deal was put in place, the FTA has unleased powerful forces which are rapidly accelerating this trend.

Meanwhile the competitive pressures created by the FTA are making it increasingly difficult for governments to raise taxes — particularly from corporations — to address the financial needs of our post-secondary institutions. Instead, both the federal government and the provinces are cutting back, while encouraging institutions to seek greater support from the private sector, as they do in the United States. Additionally, universities and colleges are being pressured to raise tuition with negative consequences for the goals of universality and accessibility.

We are also witnessing the division of universities into the U.S. pattern of elite: research-oriented institutions who continue to receive substantial public funds for commercially relevant research, and the cash-starved liberal arts faculties and universities whose financial base is being ratchetted downwards, despite growing demands for university places.

Free trade is about unleashing market forces in our society and reducing the role of government in shaping our social, economic and educational development. There is ample evidence that this is precisely what it is doing in Canada's system of post-secondary education.

Chapter Seven

Privatization Of Training: The Tory Attack On Public Training Programs

Privatization and commercialization of education is occurring not only in our primary/secondary schools and our colleges and universities, but in a wide range of publicly-funded training programs. Since its election in 1984, the federal Tory government has put in place a coherent and carefully managed strategy for shifting funding and control over training decisions to the private sector.

Canada's business community has been extremely tight-fisted in its financial support for employee training. According to a recent Statistics Canada survey, employer spending on training came to only 0.6 per cent of payroll costs. This was one quarter the level of Germany and at the bottom of the major industrialized countries. Fewer than one in three companies provide any training at all.

Instead of requiring business to redress its appalling record of failure to provide worker training, the federal government has shifted income-support funds from the unemployed to companies with training needs. Rejecting the idea of an employer payroll tax — an approach used in many other countries — the federal government has decided to make the unemployed pay for their own training, cutting back Unemployment Insurance (UI) entitlements, so that the money 'saved' can be shifted into a training fund administered by local training boards.

The privatization of training has also been promoted through redirecting money formerly paid to community colleges for training places. Instead, new arrangements have been put in place which clearly favour the use of private training institutions.

At the same time, the federal government's obsession with fiscal restraint has led to a sharp reduction in its own contributions to training. Between 1984 and 1993, the federal government's direct contribution to labour market programs fell by 45.5 per cent in real terms.[1] Moreover, a growing share of what it continues to allocate has been devoted to establishing new institutional arrangements supportive of private involvement in training, rather than the purchase of training places at public institutions.[2]

The U.S. Model Of Private-Sector Training

As with other aspects of education, Canada has differed from the United States in that public institutions have played a much larger role in training, at least until recently. Post-secondary training in the U.S. has been characterized by a relatively high proportion of private institutions. Of the 3.8-million students enrolled in training programs in 1992, 1.6-million or 42 per cent attended private career schools, 396,000 or 10 per cent attended programs sponsored by the Job Training Act and another 55,000 or 1 per cent attended two-year private programs. The total enrolment in public community college programs was 1.46-million or only 38 per cent of all post-secondary places.[3] In comparison with Canada, what is notable is the very large role of private training and the proportionately much smaller role of public programs.

The U.S. post-secondary training sector is also characterized by the activities of profit-making private educational companies, whose facilities are referred to as 'proprietary' schools. Many of the firms are small, locally-based operations with one or several schools. However, over the past two decades, large national chains have appeared handling thousands of students and collecting hundreds of millions in revenues annually.

A typical example of the chains is Phillips Colleges Inc., mentioned briefly in Chapter Six. This firm operates 91 training schools across the United States.[4] Like other proprietary school chains, Phillips makes money by tapping into federal and state training programs. It also raises revenues from tuition charged to students who enrol in its programs. The chains are basically businesses. Like businesses, they are run for the bottom line.

The encouragement of for-profit training institutions has been a deliberate policy on the part of the U.S. federal government. However, the profit motive is widely seen as responsible for major abuses of public funds, at the expense of students, staff and taxpayers.

What we have witnessed in Canada since the Tories were elected is a dramatic shift away from our tradition of publicly-funded training, towards a U.S.-style, private sector approach. Under NAFTA, these U.S. educational chains will find it much easier to move into Canada. With training being transferred to the private sector, and with U.S. firms benefitting from the right of establishment and national treatment, there will be no barriers to their rapid expansion north of the border.

The Canadian Jobs Strategy

The first major step in the Tories' privatization agenda came in September, 1985 with the announcement of the Canadian Jobs Strategy (CJS). The stated purpose of this initiative was to provide new training opportunities for Canadians to enable them to respond to the changing job market of the future. But underlying this initiative was an implicit criticism of the existing training institutions — primarily community colleges and secondary schools — as having failed to meet the training needs of industry.

Before the introduction of CJS, the federal government had helped fund community colleges by purchasing 'places' for students in the system. Federal government money was channelled directly into these provincially-operated public educational institutions. Community colleges were public institutions formally based on principles of accountability and responsiveness to community educational needs. While their governance varied from province to province, their boards of governors were normally supposed to reflect a broad cross section of community interests. (This was not always the case. In some provinces appointees were disproportionately males selected from business and professional backgrounds. But in others a broader cross-section of the commuity was given at least some representation. And there was an expectation that they be accountable to the public.)

However, once CJS was introduced, the federal government began to shift its funding from the public to the private sector. Training money was increasingly diverted from community colleges to private employers who were expected to establish their own programs or purchase training from either private training agencies or public institutions. Within three years of the new policy, fully half of federal training money which had been formerly allocated to community colleges was being diverted to private employers.[7]

This new system dramatically reduced public accountability for the money being spent while, simultaneously, giving much more control over the type, extent and quality of training to private employers. Because they were now the purchasers, private employers could make specific demands on public or private suppliers for the kind of training they needed. The needs of workers for generalized, transferable and certified training were subordinated to the job-specific interests of employers. And, the initiative provided the opportunity to bolster the development of a wide range of new private training institutions. Increasingly, training was to be privatized. In the words of two labour critics of the program, Larry Brown and Skip Kutz:

> ... [T]he Canadian Jobs Strategy wasn't about jobs at all. It was a deliberate attempt to take decisions about what training programs will be provided — and even the delivery of such programs — out of the hands of publicly-run community colleges and place them in the hands of private business. As such it is a major assault on the non-university post-secondary educational system, and a frontal attack on the fundamental assumption that education is a public responsibility.[8]

The CJS also expanded the practice of providing wage subsidies to employers as a vehicle for getting the unemployed back into the labour market. However, in the context of continuing high unemployment, this approach may simply redistribute unemployment from those who qualify for wage subsidies under the program (and therefore are attractive for employers to hire) to those not eligible for inclusion. The beneficiaries are not those who require training, but rather their employers. As Rianne Mahon notes, the government strategy's "... chosen instrument — wage subsidies — can be seen as a means for propping up low-wage employers."[9]

The Aftermath Of The 1988 Election

However, the CJS proved to be only a first step in the Tory agenda for privatizing training. Once the 1988 election was over, and the FTA ratified, Mulroney moved quickly to expand this initiative. In response to explicit election promises about providing new labour adjustment programs to workers negatively affected by free trade, the federal government established the Advisory Council on Adjustment.[13] This advisory council produced the 1989 deGrandpre Report, officially called "Adjusting to Win". The report recommended establishing a $3-billion training fund and a mandatory training tax. And it suggested major negative changes to the UI system.[11] Income replacement — the basic function of UI — was seen as a 'passive' labour market strategy. Retraining was 'active'. The policy direction should therefore be to reduce 'passive' income replacement by 'active' training measures.

The next stage was a policy paper, "Success in the Works", which was the basis of the Canadian Labour Force Development Strategy (CLFDS). This paper set out a clear agenda for increasing the role of the private sector in training, while advocating the restructuring of the UI system to eliminate 'disincentives'.[12]

The Tories then passed Bill C-21 which eliminated the federal government's $3-billion annual contribution to UI, making it a 'private' fund supported solely by employee and employer contributions. This decision brought the Canadian system into line with that in the United States.[13] It was also widely seen as directly connected to the subsidies code discussions with the

U.S., which were set up as part of the FTA. The U.S. had cited UI as a 'subsidy' which gave Canadian firms, particularly in seasonal occupations such as fishing, the ability to maintain their workforce on a year-round basis. Without UI, workers would likely abandon fishing and the industry would downsize. Thus, in the eyes of U.S. corporations Canada's unemployment insurance system enabled Canadian firms to compete 'unfairly' with U.S. firms whose workers did not receive similar benefits.[14]

Eliminating the federal government's contributions to UI would end one source of U.S. trade challenges to Canadian products.

In addition to 'privatizing' the UI fund, the federal government wanted to expand its role — and the role of business — in shaping Canada's training programs. However, it was also committed to expenditure restraint and reducing the size of the public sector. New spending on training programs was thus ruled out. So it came up with a novel source of funding: the Unemployment Insurance Fund.

Looting The Unemployment Insurance Fund

Bill C-21 permitted up to 15 per cent of the fund to be used each year — $2 billion annually — for UI training. The new Tory program envisioned transferring UI funds to private employers in the form of training grants. This new use — or what many saw as abuse — of the UI fund constituted a fundamental break with the principle of unemployment insurance as an income replacement program. It met with enormous opposition from a wide spectrum of labour, women's, anti-poverty and other advocacy organizations.

Indeed, while the Tories went through the motions of consultation, they were unable to persuade opponents of the initiative to agree to this new use of UI funds. So, they unilaterally pushed the new program through Parliament, ignoring the concerns of the trade union movement and representatives of the unemployed who saw this as the 'looting' of UI money.

The UI system was originally set up as an income support program. Its purpose was to provide workers with a pay cheque when they lost their jobs. Both employers and workers contributed to the fund which was designed to provide workers with 'insurance' protection in the event of lay-off or permanent job loss. The government guaranteed the fund's solvency by contributing money when the rate of unemployment rose during recessions.

When UI was first established, it was assumed that the government was responsible for keeping unemployment down. If it failed to do so, it had an obligation to protect workers who were the unwitting victims of its economic mismanagement. This was the rationale for the government contributing to the fund during periods of high unemployment. UI payments were also seen as a component of a Keynesian, anti-cyclical economic policy which would limit downturns in the business cycle.

However, the goal of full employment (and, indeed, even the definition of full employment) has been gradually displaced by other, neo-conservative policy objectives. Unemployment rates of 10 or 11 per cent or more are now seen as a 'normal' characteristic of our economy. But such high rates of unemployment also mean much higher levels of UI payments.

Employers have increasingly objected to the rising costs of UI (even though they have been caused by the very neo-conservative economic policies business has promoted). To cut costs and discipline the workforce, employers have demanded cuts in both the duration and amount of benefits, arguing that existing levels of benefits acted as a disincentive to work. This approach has been consistently articulated by groups such as the Canadian Federation of Independent Business, the Canadian Chamber of Commerce, the BCNI and the Canadian Manufacturers' Association.

Bill C-21 implemented much of what private employers had been calling for since the early 1980s. In the words of the Senate committee which reviewed the UI amendments:

> The motivation behind these changes appears to be not simply to divert funds to new training programs, but to promote what one witness euphemistically described as the 'adhesion' of workers to their jobs. The government would seem to believe that many of the unemployed are in a position of their own making, and that, with proper 'incentives', they would find work or remain in their jobs longer.[15]

Business interests have wanted to recoup part of their contribution to the fund. Increasingly, the income support which unemployed workers require will be tied to their willingness to meet whatever training or wage subsidy conditions employers demand.

Harmonizing To U.S. Standards

When the FTA was signed, Canada's system of unemployment insurance was far superior to that of the United States. It provided workers with 60 per cent of benefits for up to a full year of unemployment. And, in areas of high unemployment, the number of weeks of work needed to re-qualify was as low as twelve. Fully 70 per cent of the labour force was covered by UI.

In contrast, the U.S. system provides an average level of benefits of about 35 per cent of previous earnings. The duration of benefits is capped at 26 weeks, with a few exceptions such as Alaska. Worse, less than one third of the workforce is covered by the U.S. system. Moreover, within this average figure there are wide variations because the U.S. system is largely state-administered. In some states the vast majority of workers have no income protection whatsoever in the event they lose their jobs.[16]

As noted above, the Tories have drastically cut UI benefits through a variety of amendments. They have made it more difficult to qualify, reduced the duration of benefits in most parts of the country and, most recently, have passed Bill C-113 which cuts the level of benefits to 57 per cent of insurable earnings. This bill cuts off benefits entirely to employees who 'voluntarily' quit their jobs or those who are fired for 'just cause'.

Yet, at the very same time that they have ended federal contributions to UI and reduced the benefits for the unemployed, the Tories have dipped into the Unemployment Insurance Fund to pay for their new training scheme, using the 'savings' accrued from reducing benefits to the unemployed.

Overseeing The Private Project

One of the key initiatives in the privatization of training in Canada has been the new CLFDS. The Tories began this initiative shortly after they won the 1988 free-trade election. The core of this program is to shift UI funds to employers through training grants administered by provincial and local training boards. In the process it has also greatly increased the federal government's role — and the role of business — in Canada's training programs.

CLFDS was established after a two-stage process co-ordinated by the Canadian Labour Market and Productivity Centre. The first phase consisted of seven task forces on specific areas of Canada's training needs.[17] The second phase, restricted to business and labour participants, worked on implementing the labour market proposals developed in phase one. The key proposal was to set up a national training board with representation from business, labour, women's groups, educational, aboriginal nations, visible minorities and the disabled. Business and labour would be the dominant players, however. The structure of the national board would be replicated at provincial and local levels.[18]

In 1991, the Canadian Labour Force Development Board was formally set up. It has eight representatives from business, eight from labour, two from the education and training community and four from the social groups. There are also ex-officio, non-voting representatives of the federal and provincial governments.[19]

Part of the plan is to have a provincial board to supervise the use of training money in each province. Another component is to set up approximately 60 local boards (the actual number is still being debated) to oversee the administration of the program in individual communities. To date, these boards have not been established.

Plans for the new national training board and its provincial and local counterparts were based, in part, on the 'reforms' introduced by former British Prime Minister Margaret Thatcher. (The Tories were so enthusiastic about the British system — and to a lesser degree the systems in several other European countries — that they took sceptical Canadian labour officials to Europe so they could see, first hand, the benefits of the system. The junket backfired. Many Canadian trade unionists were appalled by the British system which gives employers who supervise workers on 'training' programs draconian powers over 'trainees' and which has largely excluded local governments, trade unions and community representatives from any role in allocating training money.)

Although the plans remain somewhat in flux, the federal government seems to be moving towards having local boards emerge as the key administrators of training funds. Composed equally of representatives of business, labour and the 'community', there is every reason to believe that they will quickly end up dominated by business interests — interests who, as employers, would directly benefit from the money dispensed by the boards.

Neither community groups nor labour have the resources at this level to participate effectively in the process. Workers appointed to the local boards may well end up on their own. Their role will be largely administrative, the major policy issues around training having already been determined by federal legislation. They will not be able to influence the 'big picture' policy issues. Rather, they are relegated to making decisions about who gets the money allocated to their area. They do not have back-up resources to ensure that proposals are properly examined. Indeed, many of them may have trouble even getting the time off to attend the meetings. Community representatives have similar problems.

Many weaknesses have been noted about the new program, including the problem of co-ordinating it with the existing public educational institutions already providing training.

The new training board system may give rise to serious conflicts with existing programs in secondary schools, community colleges and other post-secondary institutions. It will have to be co-ordinated with existing provincial programs. It also overlaps uneasily with existing apprenticeship programs. The program may well result in needless duplication of investment in certain types of training — training which is much better done in our public institutions. It will be very costly to administer, and this money will likely come out of the UI fund as well.

From the perspective of workers, the Tory government approach to training has many drawbacks. It is more likely to be employer-specific, so workers may not necessarily get transferable skills or appropriate certification for what they have learned. Many employers do not have the staff or the facilities to do systematic training. The boards appear likely to end up having little or no capacity to enforce standards, so workers on the program may be exploited simply as a source of cheap, subsidized labour.

This new system also lacks proper public accountability for the money given to employers. It could be abused by employers who see it simply as a wage subsidy or a way of getting back their UI contributions.

However, from the federal government's perspective, it will achieve three important goals. First, when fully implemented, it will give private employers much more control over training expenditures. Second, it will provide a suitable vehicle for the privatizing of training. The boards will make use of private training establishments, diverting money away from public institutions. And, third, it will institutionalize the ongoing looting of the UI fund by co-opting labour and social critics on the national, provincial, and local training boards. The Tories hope that once the boards are up and running (with reluctant, but nevertheless real, participation from labour, women's groups and others), there will be no turning back the clock. Once there are enough business, labour and community appointees involved on these boards, it will be politically impossible for critics to continue to demand that the money be returned to the UI fund and used exclusively for income support.

Getting The Provinces To Expand Private Training

The federal government has also entered into Labour Force Development Agreements with the provinces. In this area, it has pushed to shift resources from public to private training bodies. For example, in the agreement negotiated with British Columbia, the Canadian government demanded incremental reductions in the amounts allocated to public institutions. Clause 13.03 of the agreement reads as follows:

> Canada intends, over time, to gradually decrease its level of government-to-government purchase arrangements for training

given by public authorities of British Columbia, and to promote, through increased funding arrangements with private sector organizations, an increased role of the private sector in training. Accordingly, to assure a degree of stability to British Columbia while adjusting to the new direction, Canada undertakes to allocate and make available for government-to-government purchase arrangements for training from public authorities of British Columbia not less than:

$29,700,000 in fiscal year 1991-92
$25,700,000 in fiscal year 1992-93
$22,600,000 in fiscal year 1993-94 [20]

These reductions should be viewed in light of earlier allocations from public institutions. In 1985-86, fully $52.2 million was spent in direct training purchases in B.C. from public institutions. Only $4.8 million was allocated to private institutions in the same year. Allocations to public institutions declined steadily through the CJS Agreement with B.C. from $46.1 million in 1986-87 to $31.4 million in 1990. And the new Labour Force Development Agreement continues this trend, as noted above.

Similar provisions have been pushed by the federal government in its agreements with other provinces. What is also significant about this approach by the federal government is that it is levering provincial funding into the private sector in addition to the money that it is putting there. In other words, it is encouraging the provinces to abandon public training institutions in favour of private training providers.

Not surprisingly, the efforts of the Tory government to foster private training have led to a dramatic increase in the number of private training agencies and the number of students enrolled. For example, in B.C. there were 216 registered training institutions in 1983. By 1990, there were approximately 500. Recent estimates by the B.C. Ministry of Advanced Education indicate that the number of private training institutes will exceed 800 in 1993.[21]

In 1983, approximately 33,000 students attended private institutions. By 1990, this number had doubled to 67,000. During the same period the number of students in public colleges and institutes rose slightly as well, but the increase was at a far lower pace, rising from 54,600 to 69,600.[22] However, vocational enrolment in public colleges and institutions actually declined. While B.C. under previous Social Credit governments saw itself as a leader in promoting private education, other provinces are now "catching up" with the encouragement of the federal government.

A Coherent Plan For Privatized Training

While the Tories' new initiative is not tagged with any connection to free trade, the reality is that it is very much a part of the free trade agenda. It involves transferring educational decision-making to private employers. It establishes the skill requirements of employers as the dominant factor in shaping training policy. It undermines existing public programs by arbitrarily assuming that skills training is better carried out by private firms or private employers, than by community colleges and other public institutions.

The Tory agenda also cuts back the financial support for our public programs. In the future, community colleges will not only get less money, they will have to 'compete' with private agencies for the training dollars. And, once training is privatized, there is nothing to prevent its eventual takeover by U.S.-based training chains who will then have all the protections guaranteed under NAFTA.

The Tory training agenda is also having a major, if perhaps more subtle, impact on our public institutions. The new training board structure and the greater business voice in the allocation of money is pressuring community colleges to act if they were private institutions — sacrificing quality to win tenders, abandoning historic commitments to broad-based training in order to meet employer's desire for job-specific training and restructuring their programs to be 'competitive' with the private providers they are now forced to compete with. In short, our public institutions are being commercialized as a result of the new training environment created by the Tories.

It is not accidental that this major restructuring of training has come as part of an overall package of economic, social and educational changes implemented by a government insistent on Canadians 'adjusting' to free trade. As has been noted elsewhere, the U.S. system of funding training has a much larger private sector component. Over half the U.S. federal training money is being allocated to private training agencies. Canada is now clearly moving in this direction. If we assume that much of what has made Canada a separate and distinct country has been the extent and quality of its public programs, the privatization of training can be viewed as one more way in which Canada is being 'harmonized' and 'integrated' into the new hemispheric agenda of the United States.

Chapter Eight

NAFTA And The Public Sector

The Disastrous Decline Of Public Programs

It would be remiss to conclude without discussing the impact of NAFTA on the broader public sector, of which education is a part. Educational services in Canada have been fundamentally — and we would argue beneficially — influenced by the 'public' culture which has characterized much of Canada's mixed economy. Canada's public and social programs have been a key component of Canada's identity as a country. If these are destroyed, education falls with them.

One of the most critical concerns of Canadians during the 1988 free-trade election was whether Canada's cherished social programs would be undermined by free trade. During that election, supporters of free trade went to extraordinary lengths to assure Canadians that our social safety net and our public programs would not be adversely affected.

An ageing Dr. Emmett Hall, chair of the federal Royal Commission which recommended the establishment of medicare, was called out of retirement and asked for his views on the impact of the FTA on health care. He replied that he could find nothing in the actual text of the deal that would adversely affect medicare. (The fact that Hall had been a Tory was given little publicity by the media. He was portrayed as the "father of medicare" — a label designed to enhance his credibility, while minimizing his partisan connection to the governing Conservatives.)

Numerous economists who supported the deal ridiculed its opponents for even raising the connection between free trade and the erosion of Canada's social programs. In a popularly-written, tabloid-style newspaper insert distributed to millions of homes the day before the election, two *Financial Post* economists asserted smugly that old age pensions, family allowances, medicare and unemployment insurance were all completely safe in the new economic framework created by free trade. "Read my lips," they intoned. "No concessions on social programs."[1]

They claimed that the concerns of opponents reflected a basic ignorance of the underlying economics of freer trade. Protectionist criticisms totally misinterpreted the actual content of the deal and created unjustified fears about its consequences. Far from undermining Canada's social and public programs, they predicted that free trade would strengthen Canada's economy and, in the process, provide the resources needed to enhance Canada's social safety net. Free trade would bring jobs, investment and prosperity. A stronger, more prosperous economy would have a more solid tax base and be able to generate the money needed to maintain — indeed improve — our public and social services.

Every one of their predictions has been wrong. Old Age Pensions have been de-indexed and a claw-back provision introduced to eliminate higher-income pensioners from receiving benefits. The ratchet-like effect of these changes will be to make it impossible for Canadians to continue to rely on public pensions to provide adequate retirement income.

Universal Family Allowances — another 'sacred trust' — were eliminated in early 1993. They were replaced with a new, income-related system which provides less money to most families and whose level of benefits will erode over time because of inadequate inflation indexation. The new system is a U.S.-style, means-tested welfare scheme in which support from the middle class can be expected to diminish as their benefits evaporate. In the process, one of the few cash payments which women had a right to receive directly from the government has been abandoned.

The UI system has been ripped apart. As we noted in the previous chapter, new barriers to qualifying have been erected. The duration of benefits has been reduced. The amount of benefits as a proportion of insurable earnings has been cut. And, new punitive measures have been introduced to deny benefits entirely to workers who voluntarily quit their jobs without just cause. UI has been 'harmonized' downwards towards the U.S. model.

Even Medicare Threatened

Medicare itself is now in crisis. The massive reduction in federal transfers implemented by the Tory government has forced provinces to embark on wide-ranging health care 'reforms' designed to cope with the funding shortfall. Cash-strapped provincial governments have cut drug benefit plans, eliminated coverage for Canadians travelling outside the country, rationed non-emergency treatments and, increasingly, sought to reduce costs by privatizing services, often to multinational health care companies. The Canada Health Act, which enforces the five basic principles of medicare, will be ineffective once federal cash transfers disappear. This could happen by the end of the decade in some provinces. In short, even medicare is on the critical list.

There has, of course, been a great deal of finger-pointing to other causes of the systematic dismantling of our social safety net — the recession, an over-valued dollar, high interest rates and mounting government deficits — since free trade was enacted. But the fact remains that the free-trade environment has proved to be extremely damaging to the maintenance of public programs and services.

The bottom line is that the federal government has followed policies which are fully consistent with the predictions made by critics concerning the negative impact of the FTA on the public sector.

Although misleadingly described as trade deals, neither the FTA nor NAFTA are primarily about trade in the conventional sense. Rather, they are about establishing a new legal, regulatory and investment framework for international business — one which will protect corporate interests and guarantee a stable and predictable business climate through imposing new, and permanent, restrictions on future governments in Canada,

Mexico and, in short order, a fairly long list of IMF/World Bank-approved applicants from Central and South America.

Both deals are also about advancing the commercialization of our society: transforming culture, intellectual life and a wide variety of public programs and institutions into commodities whose value and, in some cases, very existence is determined in the marketplace.

However, due to its broadened scope, its ongoing process for inexorable extension of market principles to economic and social areas initially exempted, its potential to bring in new member countries (thereby diminishing Canada's influence in its future evolution) and its pro-active institutional and enforcement provisions, NAFTA is much more of an assault on Canada's mixed economy and its public traditions, including education, than the FTA.

The Anti-Public Sector Bias Of NAFTA

As is already evident from our analysis of the text in Chapter Two, NAFTA is designed to stop pro-active government intervention in the economy. It is also structured to reduce the use of government-operated services and programs to achieve public policy objectives. This is evident in its overall philosophical objectives and in many of its specific provisions.

NAFTA's long-term, and quite explicit, objective is to limit the ability of governments to regulate the economy, while shifting a wide range of public sector functions and services into the private marketplace, where they will become the basis of profit-making activities. Under the agreement, the value of the public sector is assessed not according to how well it meets the social, economic and cultural needs of Canadians, but rather by its contribution to the expansion and enhancement of business opportunities.

This anti-public-sector bias is reflected in the assumption — pervasive throughout the agreement — that public provision of services is inherently undesirable. Public provision of goods and services is only acceptable when unavoidable — a kind of provision of 'last resort' — in circumstances where the market cannot do it.

As was noted in the case of daycare, if a government does

decide to go ahead with a new program, it must pay full compensation for the loss of market opportunity to private firms — a feature which effectively nullifies any financial benefit which the public might enjoy as a result of the introduction of a more efficient public program. The public's savings would have to be handed over as compensation for the loss of market opportunity.[2]

Restricting Government As Manager

NAFTA also limits the ability of future governments in Canada to *manage* the economy. It forbids the use of a variety of public policy tools which, historically, have been utilized to stimulate investment and encourage firms to generate jobs in Canada. Instead, future governments will be barred from 'interfering' in the market.

As noted earlier, Chapter Ten of the NAFTA limits the use of government procurement as an industrial policy measure. In 1992, Canadian governments spent approximately $61.3 billion on purchases of goods and services. This represented about 42 per cent of their overall expenditures. They also spent another $17.5 billion on capital investment. In total, the public sector procurement market amounted to $78.8 billion in 1992.[3] NAFTA is intended to stop governments from using this purchasing to support domestic industries.

As we saw in Chapter Two, to ensure that this objective is achieved, NAFTA contains new and very detailed tendering requirements, including the kind of information which governments must provide to prospective bidders and the process which must be followed in selecting successful bidders. U.S. or Mexican companies which feel that they have lost out to local or domestic interests will be able to demand a review of the process — a review which would include the ability of the new reviewing body to require that a government award the contract to a bidder whose NAFTA rights had been violated.

Constraints On Public Sector Mandates

NAFTA also imposes a number of new constraints on the operation of the public sector, particularly with respect to the management of Crown corporations. Historically, governments have used Crown corporations to achieve a variety of economic, social, regional and political objectives. They have been a vehicle for pumping investment into depressed areas, capturing resource revenues, and providing infrastructure needed by the private sector. They have also been established to provide cheap power or other inputs to attract industry to a province or region.

Sometimes they have been set up to carry out socially desirable functions which the private sector refused to do, or did badly, such as workers' compensation or auto insurance. The point is that Canadians have viewed Crown corporations not simply as narrow economic entities, but more broadly as vehicles for achieving a variety of goals, including building the nation itself.

However, NAFTA incorporates new rules which would sharply reduce the 'non-economic' functions of Crown corporations and force them to behave exclusively on a commercial basis. Chapter Fifteen of NAFTA requires that federal Crown corporations act "solely in accordance with commercial considerations in its purchase or sale of the monopoly good or service." The agreement defines "commercial considerations" as those "consistent with the normal business practices of privately-held enterprises in the relevant business or industry."

Yet, many of our Crown corporations have service mandates. For example, hydro-electric utilities are required to provide services to citizens in rural areas where revenues may not cover costs, but where, for social reasons, it is seen as desirable for services to be provided.

Historically, many of the service mandates have been legislated because certain services were seen as a 'right' which should be accessible to all citizens, regardless of their region, place of residence or other characteristic which might make it otherwise 'uneconomic' to provide them with it. In requiring all public enterprises to operate according to market disciplines all social, regional and other redistributive functions of these enterprises will be abandoned. The new constraints which we argue are going to apply to education under NAFTA are part and parcel of this larger approach to destroying Canada's culture of 'public' institutions.

The Loss Of Provincial Jurisdiction

One of the most important areas in which NAFTA expands the FTA is in its impact on provincial and local governments. During the debate about the FTA, the full provincial implications of the deal were not extensively discussed. Some concerns were raised about the deal's impact on provincial jurisdictions, but these tended to be overshadowed by the impact on other aspects of the Canadian economy. At the same time, it has gradually emerged that the FTA has removed a number of significant provincial powers.

NAFTA clearly includes the provinces. The agreement requires the three national governments to enter into negotiations with the view to extending the provisions to state and "provincial government entities." The deadline for the conclusion of these negotiations is explicitly set out in the agreement: 1998. There is, therefore, every reason to believe that the procurement provisions of NAFTA will soon include provincial governments and their Crown corporations, subject to the (temporary) exclusions negotiated between Ottawa and the provinces.

For example, NAFTA will eventually cover the very large purchases by provincial Crown corporations, such as hydro-electric utilities. Ontario Hydro alone spent $2.24 billion on procurement of goods and services in 1992. Historically, it has followed a 'buy Canadian' policy, within a 10 per cent price guideline with respect to its purchases. In doing so, it has been able to provide a very large market to Ontario — and Canadian — industries. NAFTA will eventually end this practice. In the process, it will deny provincial governments a key lever of local economic development.

The inclusion of provincial Crown corporations will have a limiting effect in Canada disproportionate to that in the U.S. or Mexico. Canada's tradition of provincial Crown corporations is quite different from the other two countries. In the U.S., the economic role of publicly-owned enterprises operated by state governments is very limited. In Mexico, the central government has played the dominant role in setting up and operating the country's state enterprises.

Neither Mexico nor the U.S. has a comparable tradition of

using state or provincial-level Crown corporations as vehicles for economic development. In neither of these countries do states play a comparable role as major owner-operators of utilities, resource firms and insurance providers. Nor are there clear parallels to the constitutional rights of our provincial governments in this area.

Thus the implications of including provincial governments and their Crown corporations, agencies and other bodies are very different from what would occur in the U.S. or Mexico. Specifically, the inclusion means that the federal government, through the trade deal, has effectively taken over areas of constitutional responsibility which were under the exclusive jurisdiction of the provinces. The heated debates which occurred during the Charlottetown Accord process are largely academic in this context. The NAFTA has already decided whether certain powers will remain with the provinces. Neither the U.S. nor Mexico faces the same constitutional issues which confront Canada as a result of NAFTA.

Local governments are also mentioned in the deal for the first time — although in a carefully expressed manner which suggests that most local government activities will not immediately be affected by the deal. As we noted earlier, they are the legislated creations of provincial governments, rather than a constitutionally guaranteed level of government. Consequently provinces could well be pressured into requiring them to adhere to the 'disciplines' of NAFTA as well.

Much of Canada's public sector is administered at the provincial or local level. Thus, the inclusion of these levels of government is very significant for the future of our public programs and public enterprises.

From the perspective of Canada's public sector and its social programs, the incursion of NAFTA into these areas is very worrisome. Many of the issues which Canadians have traditionally assumed provincial governments are elected to deal with will be removed from their ambit.

Provincial governments also face the problem of not being signatories to the trade deal. It is signed only by federal governments. Consequently the review committees and working parties of the Free Trade Commission are composed of individuals selected by these federal governments. Provinces have no right to representation on the bodies that rule on issues which are of fundamental importance to their jurisdictions. Thus the provinces, within whose constitutional jurisdiction educational decisions are supposed to reside, are not even guaranteed a place in the negotiations which will determine the future exclusion, or inclusion, of a variety of public educational programs.

Provincial governments have the constitutional responsibility for education as well as many other key public services in Canada. Yet, as we have seen, the FTA — and even more so NAFTA — place major restrictions on the ability of provinces to operate and regulate educational services within their boundaries.

Placing Shackles On Democracy

"A trade deal simply limits the extent to which the U.S. or other signatory government may respond to pressure from their citizens."[4] This comment by Michael Walker, of the conservative Fraser Institute, goes to the heart of the issue of limiting the role of government — and democracy — in our society.

NAFTA has ramifications which go to the core of the functions of government in a democratic society. It shifts, dramatically, the boundary between what is decided by the market and what is decided by democratically-elected governments; enhancing the role of the former, while imposing many new shackles on the latter.

There is a legitimate debate over whether some decisions should be made through the marketplace or through the ballot box. However, it is quite inappropriate for one particular government to give away the rights of the electorate over a variety of decisions concerning the role of public programs in this country through an international agreement which would bind all future governments to a neo-conservative agenda.

Indeed, a very large part of NAFTA is crafted to weaken the power of government, while transforming its role from an institution which reflects popular, democratic aspirations to one of enforcing a new business agenda. Simultaneously, the deal is designed to provide a wide range of new 'rights' — and new international enforcement mechanisms — to promote multinational corporate interests.

Institutionalizing Neglect

A decade ago, Canadians travelling to the U.S. were shocked at the number of homeless people, the extent of urban decay and the enormous disparities in wealth and educational opportunity among the population. Now these same problems are appearing in all our major cities. Canada's first food bank was founded as late as 1983 and was seen as a temporary measure to deal with a short-term crisis. Now food banks are an institutionalized part of our welfare system, with hundreds of thousands of people — including children — dependent on their hand-outs. While free trade is not the only factor in such developments, there is mounting evidence that it has been critical in unleashing new and destructive economic forces.

The FTA has already resulted in major negative changes to our public and social services — changes which most Canadians abhor. NAFTA will erode much more of our public sector. It will drematically reduce our social safety net and, in the process, place enormous new strains on our public education system.

The dismantling of Canada's unique 'public sector' culture and its replacement by a U.S.-style, private, market-dominated approach to economic and social decision-making will weaken the support of our public educational system. Public education has not evolved in a vacuum. It has reflected our approach to a variety of public policy questions, including health care, broadcasting, communications, transportation, social welfare and the like. When these supporting public institutions are privatized and commercialized, it will be increasingly difficult to maintain our heritage of public education.

Education is at the core of a nation's culture and sovereignty. To reflect the aspirations and the culture of a society, educational institutions must be shaped by the collective decisions of the members of the society. In Canada this has been done through a variety of public institutions — school boards, university and college boards' of governors, provincial and federal governments and the broader educational community.

Educational policy cannot be turned over to international markets, unless the real objective is to abandon institutions that are uniquely Canadian and let them and replaced by those of a culturally aggressive economic giant next door. Free trade is about privatizing and commercializing our public sector and restructuring our society according to business values. The 'spillover' of this process to our existing system of public education will be significant. And it will occur at a rate far faster than most Canadians can, as yet, imagine. In the process, much of what is 'Canadian' about Canada will disappear.

It is time the Canadian educational community took a serious look at NAFTA, before much of what has taken generations to build in this country has been dismantled.

Notes

CHAPTER ONE

1. Government of Canada, *North American Free Trade Agreement*, Ottawa: Queen's Printer, 1992.

2. Government of Canada, *The Canada-United States Free Trade Agreement*, Ottawa: Queen's Printer, 1988. The number of articles and books analyzing the Canada-U.S. FTA is enormous, and we are in no position to cite them all. For a well-documented, but largely uncritical, account of the negotiation of the FTA see: G. Bruce Doern and Brian W. Tomlin, *Faith and Fear*, Toronto: Stoddart, 1991. The agruments supporting free trade have been made by a large number of economists including Richard Lipsey, Michael Hart, Ronald and Paul Wonnacott, Richard Harris and Alan Rugman, to cite only a few. Opponents of free trade have also written extensively and we would recommend the work of Jack Warnock, Duncan Cameron, Daniel Drache, Bruce Campbell, Mel Clarke, Mel Watkins, Stephen Clarkson and Maude Barlow.

3. A brief search through the *Canadian Journal of Education*, for example, reveals an almost total lack of interest in the impact of either the FTA or NAFTA on education. The book review section is the only area where the issue has arisen, and the coverage given to books dealing with the issue has been meagre indeed. The major exception to this generalization is to be found in the publications of the teachers' federations and other labour unions.

4. Knowledge on Demand, "News Release: North American Free Trade Agreement on Disk," Vancouver, Feb. 7, 1993; IRL Information Retrievers Ltd. 4493 Brakenridge St., Vancouver, B.C. advertising leaflet (undated), Spring, 1993. Other private companies, such as CCCH Ltd., have also been given the right to distribute the text of NAFTA. This is in contrast to the text of the FTA which was widely — and freely — distributed by the Department of External Affairs to anyone who wanted a copy.

5. Ontario Cabinet Committee on the North American Free Trade Agreement, *Final Report,* Toronto: Queen's Printer, 1993, p.1.

6. There were other, quite different reasons voiced in opposition to the side

deals by many labour, environmental and other critics of NAFTA. These focused on the inherent contradictions of attempting to 'fix' a deal whose fundamental intent was to weaken governments and empower corporations by vague commitments to respect environmental and labour rights.

7. There was a certain logic to the position of the Tories. They argued that giving the U.S. additional rights to countervail on the basis of labour or environmental practices would provide Congress with another method to extract trade concessions from Canada and Mexico. However, the argument was truly ironic in that the Tories had earlier failed to get secure access to the U.S. market under the FTA. They had accepted a watered-down disputes panel mechanism which focused on whether the U.S. was interpreting its own laws fairly, rather than on a new process which would override section Section 301 of the U.S. trade legislation.

8. The lack of public input during the passage of NAFTA and the calculated decision to deny the electorate a vote on the matter gives rise to major questions about the erosion of democracy in Canada. Indeed, since the Mulroney government was elected, Canadians have become much more cynical about the democratic process.

9. Canadian Union of Public Employees, *An Active Public Sector: Time to Challenge NAFTA,* Toronto: April 8, 1993, pp. 8–9.

CHAPTER TWO

1. Government of Canada, *The North American Free Trade Agreement,* Ottawa: Queen's Printer, 1992, Preamble.

2. *Ibid.*, Part One, General Part, Chapter One, Objectives, p. 1 — 1. Significantly, Mexico negotiated a special annex, Annex 111, which sets out a number of "Activities Reserved to the Mexican State". These include: Petroleum and Petrochemicals, Electricity, Nuclear Power, Satellite Communications, Telegraph Services, Postal Services, Railroads, Minting Coins and a variety of government inspection services. The Tories did not see it necessary to protect any state activity from the provisions of the agreement under this annex.

3. NAFTA, Article 1202: National Treatment

4. NAFTA, Article 1202: National Treatment

5. NAFTA, Article 1205: Local Presence

6. This example could also be dealt with under the procurement provisions of NAFTA in as much as it deals with a service tendered by a government. It would also fit under the investment chapter under certain conditions, such as when a Canadian firm holding a service contract was bought out by a U.S. firm. However, it is our view that it also fits under the services chapter by virtue of the national treatment and local presence provisions of that chapter. Once procurement is fully applicable at the provincial level, the rules it

imposes will be even more stringent. As we discuss later, the tendering process will be structured according to new international rules which will make it far easier for U.S. firms to apply for procurement contracts.

7. *Globe and Mail*, Feb. 23, 1993.

8. The School of Education, University of Southern California, the Southern California Field Office, Educational Testing Service, "The Educational Impact of the North American Free Trade Agreement: A Proposal to Support a Conference Between Educators in the United States, Canada and Mexico", San Diego: March, 1992, p.5.

9. NAFTA Article 1001: Scope and Coverage. It should be mentioned that the lower $25,000 (US) threshold for goods incorporated in the Canada-U.S. FTA has been 'grandparented' under Annex 1001.2c: Country Specific Thresholds. The Canada-U.S. provisions apply until January 1, 1994 after which they will be folded into the NAFTA.

10. NAFTA Article 1024: Further Negotiations.

11. NAFTA Chapter 15, Annex 1505: Country Specific Definitions of State Enterprises. The wording explicitly includes provincial Crown corporations.

12. It is interesting to note that in the U.S., universities and business lobbied strenuously to change the federal government's policies regarding patents arising from federally-funded research. Instead of ruling that such rights be owned by the taxpayers, a 1980 change in patent laws gave automatic ownership to universities. (It is useful to remember that many U.S. universities are private, so this also entailed the privatization of ownership of the results of publicly-funded research.) This change enabled universities to licence patents to business. As David Noble points out: "This prompted a reworking of academic policies regarding intellectual property in the interest of profit-making and paved the way for a massive indirect public subsidy of private industry via the universities." David Noble, "Higher Education Takes the Low Road," *Newsday*, Oct. 8, 1989.

13. At the time of writing, Bill C-62, the Telecommunications Act, is still under consideration, but it would replace major components of the Railway Act. It is listed in Annex 1310 "Conformity Assessment Procedures".

14. Barry Duncan, "TV Inc. in the Classroom," O.S.S.T.F. *Education Forum*, Fall, 1992, p. 18.

15. *Ibid.*, p. 20.

CHAPTER THREE

1. Report of the Education Task Force, *Restructuring Public Education: Building a Learning Community*, Washington Education Association, p. 9.

2. Joel H. Spring, *Education and the Rise of the Corporate State*, Boston: Beacon Press, 1972, p. 151.

3. *Ibid.*, p. 61.

4. Clarence J. Karier, "Business Values and the Educational State," in *Schooling and Capitalism: A Sociological Reader*, London: Routledge & Kegan Paul, 1976, p. 21.

5. Spring, *op cit.*, p. 51.

6. William E. Coffman, "A King Over Egypt, Which Knew Not Joseph," *Education Measurement — Issues and Practice*, Summer, 1993, p. 6.

7. Spring, *op cit.*, p. 60.

8. Patricia A. Graham, "What America Has Expected of Its Schools over the Past Century," *American Journal of Education*, February 1993, p. 92.

9. *Ibid.*, p. 87.

10. National Commission on Excellence in Education, *A Nation at Risk*, April, 1983, p. 5.

11. Carol A. Ray and Roslyn A. Mickelson, "Restructuring Students for Restructured Work: The Economy, School Reform, and Non-college-bound Youths," *Sociology of Education*, January, 1993, p. 4.

12. *Ibid.*, p. 4.

13. *Ibid.*, p. 7.

14. *Ibid.*, p. 9.

15. *Ibid.*, p. 9.

16. Ad Hoc Committee on Education, "The Role of Business in Education Reform: Blueprint for Action", April, 1988.

17. "What the Roundtable Is, Why It Was Founded, How It Works," *Business Roundtable*, (photocopy) July, 1990.

18. Ad Hoc Committee on Education, *op. cit.*, p. 2.

19. *Ibid.*, p. 17.

20. Don T. Martin, "The Political Economy of School Reform in the United States," *Understanding Educational Reform in Global Context*, New York: Garland, 1991, p. 354.

21. *Ibid.*, p. 361.

22. Alex Molnar, "Fears about Business Involvement," *Rethinking Schools*, Autumn, 1992, p. 7.

23. Larry Cuban, "The Corporate Myth of Reforming Public Schools," *Phi Delta Kappan*, October, 1992, p. 157.

24. *Ibid.*, p. 159.

25. Harold Howe II, "America 2000: A Bumpy Ride on Four Trains," *Phi Delta Kappan*, November, 1991, p. 198.

26. Denis P. Doyle, "America 2000," *Phi Delta Kappan*, November, 1991, p. 186.

27. Robert Lowe, "The Hollow Promise of School Vouchers," *False Choices (Rethinking Schools Special Issue)*, 1992, p. 3.

28. Daniel Weinstraub, "Savings Could Exceed Cost of School Voucher Program," *Los Angeles Times*, July 22, 1993, pp. A1–A2.

29. Ira Emery Rodd, "McLunchrooms!," *The Nation*, Sept. 21, 1992, p. 276.

30. Alex Molnar, *op. cit.*, p. 7.

31. "Programs to Destroy Public Education," *American Labour*, 1986, p. 2.

32. Michael Apple, *Official Knowledge: Democratic Education in a Conservative Age*, New York: Routledge, 1993, p. 100.

33. Douglas Noble, "The Regime of Technology in Education," *Holistic Education Review*, 1993.

34. Barbara Miner, "Education for Sale?: For-Profit Firms Target Public Schools," *Rethinking Schools*, Summer, 1993, p. 17.

35. *Ibid.*, p. 17.

CHAPTER FOUR

1. Noel F. McGinn, "Implications for Eduction of Economic Integration Within the Americas", Harvard University, Unpublished Manuscript, March 19, 1991, p.1.

2. Juan Castillas, Garcia de Leon, *The Process of Change in Higher Education in Mexico*, (unpublished paper), Mexico City: May, 1992, Table 1. (Castillas is the Executive General Secretary of the National Association of Universities and Institutions of Higher Education (ANNUIES) in Mexico.) Castillas cites his source for the data in this and the following paragraphs as the Ministry of Education.

3. *Ibid.*, Table 1.

4. *Ibid.*, Table 2.

5. *Ibid.*, Table 1.2. Percentages calculated from data in the table.

6. Jesus Martin Del Campo, "Teachers' Congress: Report on its Outcome" This is a shortened version of an article printed in *Memoria* no. 41. April, 1992, p. 7. Strangely, there seem to be quite disparate estimates of the actual membership of the union, with other authorities citing numbers from half a million upwards. In any event, the dominant role of the SNTE as the official representative of teachers is widely acknowledged.

7. *Ibid.*, p. 7.

8. The use of the expression "took power" is deliberate: there is a great deal of evidence that Salinas won the election in 1988 by massive electoral fraud. Cuauhtemoc Cardeneas, his principal opponent, was leading comfortably according to the computerized system which had been put in place for the first time to count the ballots. Mysteriously, half-way through the count on election night, the computer broke down and the ballots had to be counted by hand. Miraculously, Salinas, who had been far behind, emerged with 52 per cent of the vote — an outcome which has strained the credibility of most

independent observers. Subsequently, the governing PRI moved to burn the ballots, so no one will ever be able to recount the result and confirm, or deny, that Salinas won by massive electoral fraud.

9. Matt Witt, "Mexican Labour: The Old, the New and the Democratic," *Multi-National Monitor*, Jan./Feb., 1991, p. 33.

10. *Ibid.*, p. 33.

11. McGinn and Street note that previous presidents had attempted, at various times, to limit the growth of educational expenditures. Gustavo Diaz Ordaz, president from 1964 to 1970, cut the rate of growth of university funding from 16.5 per cent to 6.6 per cent. This attempt to limit the growth of the education budget was a factor in the 1968 riots and subsequent police repression of students. In reaction to this experience, the next president, Luis Echeverria Alvarez (1970-1976) greatly increased funding. However, his successor, Jose Lopez Portillo reversed course partly as a result of the devaluation of the peso in 1976. His policy was to stop the growth of educational expenditures, which he achieved. However, none of these earlier presidents adopted the kind of radical restructuring of education which began to be implemented by the de Madrid and Salinas governments. See: Noel F. McGinn and Susan L. Street, *Higher Education Policies in Mexico*, Office for Public Sector Studies, Institute of Latin American Studies, Austin, Texas: The University of Texas, 1980, pp. 2–3.

12. Hugo Aboites, "Economic Globalization and the Transformation of the Mexican University", a paper presented at the Future of Public Education in North America Conference, Olympia, Washington State, Jan 29–31, 1993, p. 1.

13. We are grateful to the comments of Maria Teresa Gutierrez on this point.

14. La Jornada, May 15, 19, 24, 25, 26, 28, 1992, as translated and reported in the *North American Worker to Worker Network: Free Trade Mailing*, Aug. 31, 1992, p. 15.

15. *Ibid.*, p. 15.

16. *Ibid.*, p. 15.

17. Aboites, *op cit.*, p. 7.

18. *La Jornada, op. cit.*, p. 16.

19. *Ibid.*, p. 16.

20. John Ross, "Conflicts over Mexican Ejido Continues," *Latin-America Press*, Dec. 24, 1992. Ross cites another study which estimates that the number of Mexican corn farmers will fall from 5 million to 700,000 as a result of these changes.

21. Aboites, *op cit.*, pp. 7–8.

22. John Dillon (Ecumenical Coalition on Social Justice), personal letter, July 27, 1993.

23. For a good summary of the growth of both public and private universities in Mexico see: Daniel C. Levy, *Higher Education and the State in Latin*

America: Private Challenges to Public Dominance, Chicago: University of Chicago Press, 1986, ch. 4.

24. McGinn and Street, *op cit.*, p. 1.

25. Levy, *op. cit.*, ch. 4.

26. Aboites, *op. cit.*, p. 16. A similar conclusion is drawn by Levy: "Overall, then, Mexico's public (university) sector is characterized by a wide distribution of power at many different levels, while its private sector concentrates power much more at the university-wide level, in conjunction with its sponsors. The latter parallels many hierarchical U.S. liberal arts colleges more than Mexico's public institutions parallel patterns found in U.S. public institutions. Mexico's public universities are not run by state governments as in the U.S., nor by the national government to the extent seen in modern authoritarian regimes, nor by university-wide administrations as in the U.S. or Mexican private universities, nor by senior, chaired professors as in the Continental model, nor by students to the extent found in Latin America's truly co-governmental universities, nor by workers. Instead, each of these layerings shares power. On the other hand, this means that the national government, students, and workers are far more influential in Mexican public universities than in U.S. public or private ones." Levy, *op.cit.*, pp. 142–143.

27. Gregory Katz, "Bargain University Unravels at Seams," *Dallas Morning News*, March 6, 1992.

28. *Ibid.*, March 6, 1992.

29. Alan Adelman, "Exploring An Academic Common Market in North America" *Educational Record*, Fall, 1992, pp. 35–36.

30. Jaime Tacher y Samarel, "Mexico: Yesterday, Today and Tomorrow", a paper presented to the Border Conference on Education, Oct. 8, 1991, p. 3.

31. *Ibid.*, p.3; Aboites, *op. cit.*, pp. 20–24.

32. Adelman, *op. cit.*, pp. 35–36.

33. *La Jornada*, June 25, 1990, p. 1. Cited by Aboites, *op. cit.*, p. 23.

34. Adelman, *op. cit.*, p. 36.

35. *The Chronicle of Higher Education*, June 5, 1991, p. A30.

36. *Ibid.*, p. A30.

37. Noel F. McGinn, "Implications for Education of Economic Integration Within the Americas", Boston: Harvard Institute for International Development, March 19, 1993, p. 9. I have borrowed extensively from the analysis presented in this paper in the following discussion and am indebted to Prof. McGinn's work in this area.

38. *Ibid.*, pp. 9–11.

39. *Ibid.*, pp. 11–12.

40. *Ibid.*, p. 12.

41. *Ibid.*, p. 15.

42. *Ibid.*, p. 21.
43. *Ibid.*, p. 20.
44. *Ibid.*, p. 21.

CHAPTER FIVE

1. David Langille, "The Business Council on National Issues and the Canadian State," *Studies in Political Economy*, 24, Autumn 1987, p. 49.

2. *Ibid.*, p. 56.

3. *Ibid.*, p. 69.

4. Michael Porter, "Canada at the Crossroads: The Reality of a New Competitive Environment", Ministry of Supply and Services, Canada, 1991, pp. 89–91.

5. Maryann McLaughlin, "Employability Skills Profile: What Are Employers Looking For?," *The Conference Board of Canada*, Report 81-82-E, p. 2.

6. W. N. Kissick, "Business must help cure our educational failure," *Canadian Speeches*, June/July, 1990.

7. McLaughlin, *op. cit.*, p. 4.

8. *Ibid.*, p. 3.

9. Corporate-Higher Education Forum, "To Be Our Best: Learning for the Future", Montreal, 1991.

10. Richard Pinet and Jim Sands, "What Facts, Whose Arguments?: The Globe and Mail's Portrayal of Debates about Public Education in Canada," Vancouver: B.C. Teachers' Federation, 1993, p. 9.

11. "OECD External Examiners' Report on Educational Policy in Canada", *Canadian Association for Adult Education*, 1975, p. 3.

12. *Ibid.*, p. 2.

13. *Ibid.*, p. 3.

14. Prosperity Secretariat, Government of Canada, "Learning Well...Living Well," Ottawa: Queen's Printer, 1991, p. vii.

15. *Ibid.*, p. vii.

16. *Ibid.*, p. 17.

17. *Ibid.*, p. vii.

18. *Ibid.*, p. x.

19. *Ibid.*, p. 18.

20. Jennifer Lewington, "Perceptions About Education: Hit or Myth," *Globe and Mail* — A Guide to Education (special section), August 5, 1993.

21. Geraldine Gilliss, "Length of Japanese School Year Exaggerated," Link, Canadian Teachers' Federation, December 91–January 92.

22. "The Need for Critical Thinking: The Case of Education, the Economic Council of Canada and the Media," *Professional Perspectives*, Regina: Saskatchewan Teachers' Federation, April, 1993, p. 2.

23. *Ibid.*, p. 2.

24. Andrew Jackson, "Job Losses in Canadian Manufacturing: 1989–91", Ottawa: *Canadian Centre for Policy Alternatives*.

25. "Social Policy Index," *Social Policy*, Summer, 1992, p. 7.

26. Wilfred Brown, *North American Free Trade: Implications for Canada and for Canadian Education*, p. 6.

27. *Ibid.*, p. 7.

28. *Ibid.*, p. 6.

29. *Ibid.*, p. 8.

30. *Ibid.*, p. 8.

31. Holley Knaus, "The Commercialized Classroom," *Multinational Monitor*, March, 1992, p. 14.

32. Michelle Hibler, "Classroom Commercials," *Canadian Consumer*, Sept.–Oct., 1991, p. 8.

33. *Ibid.*, pp. 8–9.

34. Gord Ekelund, "Ethics and the Corporate Classroom," *Education Forum*, Winter, 1993.

35. Hibler, *op. cit.*, p 11. Apparently, it was slated to be discontinued because the number of labels required to get a computer was so high that many schools became disillusioned and abandoned it, after having failed to meet the target.

CHAPTER SIX

1. Howard Buchbinder and Janice Newson, *The University Means Business: Corporations and Academic Work*, Toronto: The Garamond Press, 1988. We are greatly indebted to the work of Buchbinder, Newson and David F. Noble in developing the analysis presented in this chapter. Another, earlier work which documents the role of corporations in Ontario universities is: Paul Axelrod, *Scholars and Dollars: Politics, Economics and the Universities of Ontario 1945 — 1980*, Toronto: University of Toronto Press, 1982 (see especially chapters 2 and 3). From the perspective of promoting greater corporate involvement in post-secondary education, the 1984 report of the Ontario Tory-appointed Bovey Commission provided a blueprint for new 'partnerships' between business and universities. And, more recently, the Premier's Council, established by former Liberal Premier David Peterson, published a number of key documents such as *People and Skills in the New Global Economy*, Toronto: Queen's Printer, 1988. The arguments for competitiveness, retraining and making education more relevant to the economic needs of the province can be

seen as pushing forward the ethos of free trade in the educational sector.

2. Some of the changes which have occurred in post-secondary education since the FTA was originally recommended by the 1985 MacDonald Commission. Of course, it was the MacDonald Commission which provided the major justification for Mulroney's 'leap of faith' to negotiate free trade with the United States. See: *Royal Commission on the Economic Union and Development Prospects for Canada*, Ottawa: Ministry of Supply and Services, 1985, 3 vols.

3. David N. Smith, *Who Rules the Universities?*, New York: Monthly Review Press, 1974, ch. 5.

4. *Ibid.*, ch. 5 and 7.

5. David F. Noble, "Hijacking Higher Education", *Our Schools/Our Selves*, Jan/Feb., 1993, p. 8; David F. Noble, "The Multinational Multiversity," *Z Magazine*, April, 1989, p. 18.

6. Noble, "Hijacking Higher Education", *op. cit.*, p. 8.

7. *Ibid.*, p. 8. In the *Z Magazine* article cited above, Noble notes that the BHEF has been very active politically since its foundation, primarily in support of deregulation, tax cuts for business and eliminating trade barriers. "In the interests of enhancing U.S. competitive capabilities, the BHEF has fought against environmental, health and safety, land use and anti-trust legislation, as well as anything resembling 'national economic planning' and 'income redistribution'. With its distinctly multinational orientation, the BHEF has also vigorously opposed 'export controls' and 'trade barriers' of any kind as well as restrictive plant closing legislation, not to mention any policies that might encourage 'unrealistic wage and benefit' demands by 'rank and file workers'." p. 18.

8. David F. Noble, "Higher Education Takes the Low Road," *Newsday*, Oct. 8, 1998.

9. The Career Training Centre, "A Profile of the National Labour Market and Implications for American Education", Jan., 1992, as cited in *Community College Week*, Vol. 5, No. 10, Dec. 21, 1992.

10. Ed Wiley III, "Federal Indictments Rain Down on Proprietary School Chain, Others," *Community College Week*, Vol. 5, No. 10, Dec. 21, 1992, pp. 1–5.

11. *Community College Week*, Dec. 21, 1992, p. 5.

12. Wiley, *op. cit.*, p. 5.

13. Wiley, *op. cit.*, p. 1.

14. *Ibid.*, p. 5. Since this was written, other abuses have come to light. U.S. Education Department Inspector General James B. Thomas issued a report criticizing the awarding of $725 million in grants to private proprietary schools for the training of 96,000 cosmetologists in 1990. The money was given out even though there was an "oversupply" already in the profession. The report also documented non-arms length relationships between funding

organizations and private schools and a number of instances of fraud of public funds. Ed Wiley III, "Education Department Releases a Negative Report on Proprietary Schools," *Community College Week*, July 5, 1993.

15. B. Denise Hawkins, "Proprietary Schools Continue to Meet the Educational and Employment Needs of Many Disadvantaged Students," *Community College Week*, Vol. 5, No. 10, Dec. 21, 1992, p. 6. It was not until 1972 that proprietary schools were only permitted to receive U.S. federal Basic Educational Opportunity Grants.

16. This occurred dramatically, with then Finance Minister John Turner's famous budget in the autumn of 1975. This budget consciously adopted a policy of fiscal restraint. It was also accompanied by the imposition of wage and price controls to curb inflation and a variety of other measures designed to curb the growth of government programs.

17. John Calvert, *Government Limited*, Ottawa: The Canadian Centre for Policy Alternatives, 1983.

18. Claire Polster, "Partners in Crime: The Role of Government and its Agencies," *Our Schools/Our Selves*, Vol. 4, No. 2, Jan/Feb., 1993, pp. 53–54.

19. Michael Locke, "The Decline of Universities with the Rise of Edubis" (i.e. Education-Business — authors), *Society*, May, 1990, as cited by Janice Newson, "The Decline of Faculty Influence: Confronting the Effects of the Corporate Agenda", Canadian Association of Sociology and Anthropology Meetings, Victoria, B.C., May 26–31, 1990, p. 2.

20. David Scheffel, "In My Opinion," *University Affairs*, Feb., 1989, p. 20.

21. This appears to be the fate of the School of Journalism at the University of Western Ontario. Faced with a cash crisis, the university concluded that the easiest way to downsize was simply to terminate the whole program, which is only one of six such faculties in English-speaking Canada. Aside from its assertion that fiscal necessity dictated the decision, another matter raised was that the 'market' for journalism graduates had deteriorated, leading to excess supply and therefore reducing the need for journalism graduates. See Jennifer Lewington, "Pondering Which Classes to Cut," *Globe and Mail*, July 24, 1993, p. A5.

22. *Ibid.*, p. 2–3.

23. Newson, *op. cit.*, p. 2.

24. Polster, *op. cit.*, p. 56.

25. *Ibid.*, p. 56.

26. John Harris, "Universities for Sale," *This Magazine*, Vol. 25, No. 3, Sept., 1991, p. 14.

27. Harris, *op. cit.*, p. 16.

28. John Huot, "Implications of Corporate Involvement in Ontario's Community Colleges", unpublished paper presented at the Education Worker's

Seminar, Toronto, Oct. 2-3, 1991, p. 4.

29. Harris, *op. cit.*, p. 15.

30. Harris, *op. cit.*, p. 16.

31. Arthur May, "Future Chop," *The Ottawa Citizen*, July 12, 1993, p. A 7. See also Polster, "Partners in Crime", *op. cit.*, p. 54.

32. May, *op. cit.*, p. 54.

33. *Ibid.* May's article was written to defend the program from rumours that the federal government may scale it back.

34. Mair Zamir, "Which of Our Three Research Councils Will Lead Us Into This Awesome Future", *University Affairs*, Feb., 1989, p. 21.

35. Doug Saunders, "Space Academy Inc.: Building For Canada's University on the Final Frontier", *Our Schools/Our Selves,* Sept., 1992, pp. 26-40.

36. *Ibid.*, p. 30.

37. *Ibid.*, p. 28.

38. *Vancouver Sun*, Oct. 23, 1991.

39. *Ibid.*

40. *Ibid.*

41. Innovations Foundation, information profile leaflet, undated.

42. Maude Barlow and David Noble, "Science Sells Out to Low Bid: Taxpayers Finance Most of the Medical Research But Get No Reward," *Toronto Star*, June 29, 1993.

43. *Ibid.*

44. *Ibid.*

45. *The Ubyssey*, March 31, 1993.

46. Barlow and Noble, *op. cit.*

47. Harris, *op. cit.*, p. 16.

48. The following is a list the key publications released over the past decade: *Partnership For Growth* (1984); *Spending Smarter* (1985); *Making the Match* (1986); *From Patrons to Partners* (1987); *Going Global* (1988); *To Be Our Best* (1991); *Learning Goals for K-12 Education* (1992); *Investing in People: Learning For Continuous Improvement* (1992).

49. Corporate-Higher Education Forum, *Spending Smarter (Update)*, Montreal: May, 1986, Article 15, p. 16.

50. *Ibid.*, p. 16.

51. The Business Council on National Issues, *Building a New Century Economy: The Canadian Challenge*, Ottawa: March, 1993, p. 58.

52. *Ibid.*, p. 59.

53. *Ibid.*, p. 58.

54. For a very good discussion of the role of the BCNI in shaping Canada's

economic and social policies in recent years see: David Langille, "The Business Council on National Issues and the Canadian State," *Studies in Political Economy*, No. 24, Autumn, 1987, pp. 41–85.

55. Madelaine Drohan, "Home Alone" Toronto *Globe and Mail*, July 10, 1993. Section D, p. 1. Drohan goes on to document the massive cuts which the Tory government has made to Canada's overseas diplomatic posts. Ten years ago Canada had 124 diplomatic posts in 85 countries. Now it has 106 posts in 77 countries and every budget brings further cuts. The budget of Radio Canada International — a key disseminator of information about Canada — was reduced in 1984 and again in 1990. In 1991 it was slashed from $21 million to $13.5 million, a decision which resulted in half the staff being laid off. At the same time Canada's contribution to U.S.-led United Nations peacekeeping missions has risen dramatically as Canadians take a leading role in these military interventions.

56. "Statement of the Conference on North American Higher Education Co-operation: Identifying the Agenda", Racine, Wisconsin, Sept. 12–15, 1992. This is commonly referred to as the "Wingspread Conference". See also: Alan Adelman and Patricia Somers, "Exploring An Academic Common Market in North America," *Educational Record*, Fall, 1992, p. 36.

57. Wingspread Conference Proceedings, *op. cit.*

58. Adelman and Somers, *op. cit.*, p. 36.

59. *Ibid.*, p. 33. In fact, this is actually the title of their article.

60. *Ibid.*, p. 37.

61. U.S. Information Agency, "Five to Serve on Higher Education Task Force", Press Release No. 124–92, Nov. 20, 1992.

CHAPTER SEVEN

1. Marcie Cohen,"Report to the Second Annual Consultation", Women's Reference Group: Advisory Body to the Women's Representative on the Canadian Labour Force Development Board, Toronto: June, 1993, p. 2.

2. *Ibid.*, p. 2.

3. The Career Training Centre, "A Profile of the National Labour Market and Implications for American Education", Jan., 1992, as cited in *Community College Week*, Vol. 5, No. 10, Dec. 21, 1992.

4. Ed Wiley III, "Federal Indictments Rain Down on Proprietary School Chain, Others", *Community College Week*, Vol. 5, No. 10, Dec. 21, 1992, pp. 1–5.

5. Wiley, *op. cit.*, p. 5.

6. Wiley, *op. cit.*, p. 1.

7. Larry Brown and Skip Kutz, "Public Funding and Private Training. The Canadian Jobs Strategy: Privatizing Our College System," *Our Schools/Our Selves*, Dec., 1989, p. 46.

8. *Ibid.*, p. 45.

9. Rianne Mahon, "Adjusting to Win? The New Tory Training Initiative," *How Ottawa Spends*, 1991/92 ed. Bruce Doern, Ottawa: Carleton University Press, 1992, p. 85.

10. *Ibid.*, p. 85. Mahon suggests that the very close election win and the high-profile promises extracted from Mulroney during the election to provide the best labour adjustment programs in the world pushed the newly-elected government into taking these new initiatives so that it could at least make the claim that it was fulfilling this commitment.

11. Roseanne Moran, "Labour Market Training Issues", a paper prepared for the Coalition For Post-Secondary Education Conference, Nov. 13–15, 1992, p. 4.

12. "Success in the Works — A Policy Paper", Ottawa: Minister of Supply and Services, April, 1989, p. 5. as cited by Moran, *op. cit.*, pp. 4–5.

13. Mahon, *op. cit.*, p. 85.

14. Since the Mulroney government was elected there has been a systematic attack on Canada's UI system. When the Tories came to power, workers received 60 per cent of their insurable earnings for up to a maximum of 52 weeks, depending on the area of the country in which they resided.

In 1985, The Unemployment Insurance Commission changed how vacation pay and severance pay were treated by establishing Regulation 57. This change denied benefits entirely to workers with large severance pay-outs. It also delayed — and in many cases reduced — benefits to workers with smaller severance or vacation and pay-outs.

Regulation 58 was brought in by the Commission. This treated pension pay-outs as earnings and thus reduced the UI payments to workers receiving such benefits.

In 1989, Bill C-21 was introduced. It brought in a number of negative changes, including increased qualifying periods; shorter duration of benefits; increases in the maximum period of disqualification of benefits for workers who voluntarily 'quit' their jobs from 6 to 12 weeks; and a reduction in benefits to 50 per cent for 'quitters'. Bill C-21 was held up in the Senate during the famous Goods and Services Tax battle of 1990, but was finally passed in November of that year. The government estimated that it would produce savings due to reduced benefit pay-outs, of $1.3 billion annually.

Bill C-21 also included provisions for channelling through UI the 'savings' made by cutting benefits into training. It thus constituted a major break from UI's historic income support functions.

In 1992, the Tories introduced Bill C-105 (subsequently replaced by Bill C-113). This bill contained a new and extremely punitive approach to workers who 'voluntarily quit' their jobs without just cause: it denied them benefits entirely. It also reduced the maximum UI benefit level to 57 per cent of insurable earnings. The 'savings' in benefits not paid out were estimated to amount to $850 million in 1993–94 and $1.6 billion in 1994–95.

Cumulatively, these changes add up to a dramatic reduction in the UI 'safety net'. Unemployed workers now face the prospect of lower benefits, of shorter duration, reduced further by any vacation, severance or pension pay out they receive. And workers who quit their jobs face the prospect of no benefits at all.

15. "Final Report of the Senate Committee on Bill C-21", p. 14, as cited by Mahon, *op. cit.*, p. 86.

16. George E. Brown, William Gold and John Cavenagh, "Making Trade Fair," *World Policy Journal*, Spring, 1992, p. 321.

17. A list of the participants in each is included in Mahon's article.

18. Moran, *op. cit.*, pp. 5–6.

19. *Ibid.*, p. 7.

20. Canada/British Columbia Labour Force Development Agreement, pp. 29–30.

21. Data supplied by Roseanne Morin of the College Institute Educators Association of B.C.

22. *Ibid.*

CHAPTER EIGHT

1. Andrew Coyne and Bill Watson, "Everything You Wanted to Know About Free Trade, But No One's Telling You", *A Financial Post Special Report* (Compiled for the Ottawa Sun), Sunday, Nov. 20, 1988.

2. This process of 'listing' itself is likely to lead to major conflicts between the federal and provincial governments. At worst, the federal government could refuse to list certain provincial programs. Or, it could use its power to list such programs as a bargaining chip with the provinces, demanding that some be opened up, in exchange for exempting others. There is no reason to assume that the provinces will themselves be in full agreement with each other on what should be exempt. So a lowest-common-denominator approach may be the only compromise achievable. This would lead to the weakest level of protection of current public services. And it is a very real possibility.

3. Andrew Jackson, *Notes for a Presentation on NAFTA and Government Procurement Policies to the City of Toronto Forum on NAFTA*, Toronto: Canadian Labour Congress, April 28, 1993, p.1. Jackson also notes that 19 per cent of the public sector market was federal, 33 per cent was provincial, 31 per cent was local and 15 per cent was hospitals.

4. Michael Walker, Fraser Institute, as cited in "NAFTA: A New Economic Constitution", Canadian Union of Public Employees, Feb. 3, 1993.

Other Books Available From Our Schools/Our Selves

Educating Citizens: A Democratic Socialist Agenda For Canadian Education by Ken Osborne. A coherent curriculum policy focussed on "active citizenship." Osborne takes on the issues of a "working-class curriculum" and a national "core" curriculum: what should student's know about Canada and the world at large? (Issue #2)

Making A People's Curriculum: The Experience Of La maîtresse d'école edited with an introduction by David Clandfield. Since 1975 this Montreal teacher collective has been producing alternative francophone curricula on labour, human rights, peace, and geo-political issues in a framework of cooperative learning. This is an anthology of their best work. (Issue #5)

Claiming An Education: Feminism and Canadian Schools by Jane Gaskell, Arlene McLaren, Myra Novogrodsky. This book examines "equal opportunity," what students learn about women, what women learn about themselves and what has been accomplished by women who teach, as mothers and teachers. (Issue #7)

It's Our Own Knowledge: Labour, Public Education & Skills Training by Julie Davis et al. The clearest expression yet of Labour's new educational agenda for the 1990s. It begins with working-class experience in the schools and community colleges, takes issue with corporate initiatives in skills training, and proposes a program "for workers, not for bosses." (Issue #8)

Heritage Languages: The Development And Denial Of Canada's Linguistic Resources by Jim Cummins and Marcel Danesi. This book opens up the issue of teaching heritage languages in our schools to a broad audience. It provides the historical context, analyzes opposing positions, examines the rationale and research support for heritage language promotion, and looks at the future of multiculturalism and multilingualism in Canada. (Issue #10)

What Our High Schools Could Be: A Teacher's Reflections From The 60s To The 90s by Bob Davis. The author leads us where his experience has led him — as a teacher in a treatment centre for disturbed children, in an alternative community school, in a graduate education faculty, and for 23 years in two Metro Toronto high schools. The book ranges from powerful description to sharp analysis — from sex education to student streaming to the new skills mania. (Double Issue #12-13)

Cooperative Learning And Social Change: Selected Writings Of Célestin Freinet edited and translated by David Clandfield and John Sivell. Célestin Freinet (1896-1966) pioneered an international movement for radical educational reform through cooperative learning. His pedagogy is as fresh and relevant today as it was in his own time, whether dealing with the importance of creative and useful work for children or linking schooling and community with wider issues of social justice and political action. This translation is the first to bring a broad selection of Freinet's work to an English-speaking audience. (Issue #15)

Teaching For Democratic Citizenship by Ken Osborne. In this book Osborne extends his work in *Educating Citizens* and takes us through the world of modern pedagogies and the most recent research on effective teaching. He focuses particularly on "discovery learning," "critical pedagogy," and "feminist pedagogy" — drawing from a wide range of classroom practice — and builds on this foundation the key elements of an approach to teaching in which democratic citizenship is the core of student experience. (Double Issue #19-20)

Their Rightful Place: An Essay On Children, Families and Childcare in Canada by Loren Lind and Susan Prentice. The authors examine the complex ways we view our children in both private and public life and the care we give them inside our families and within a network of private and public childcare. They also offer an historical perspective on families and childcare in Canada and propose a strategy to develop "a free, universally accessible, publicly-funded, non-compulsory, high quality, non-profit, community-based childcare system" right across the country. (Issue #22)

Stacking The Deck: The Streaming Of Working Class Kids In Ontario Schools by Bruce Curtis, D.W. Livingstone & Harry Smaller. This book examines the history and structure of class bias in Ontario education. It looks at both elementary and secondary schooling and proposes a new deal for working class children. The evidence is taken from the Ontario system, but the ideas and analysis can be extended to every school in Canada. (Issue #24)

Training For What? Labour Perspectives On Job Training by Nancy Jackson et al. In this book a number of union activists analyze the corporate training agenda in Canada and open up a labour alternative. They let us see training as a tool of political struggle in the workplace, which can contribute to skill recognition, to safe and satisfying working conditions, to career progression and to building a more democratic vision of working life. (Issue #26)

Schools And Social Justice by R.W. Connell. Throughout this broad analysis, which spans the educational systems of Europe, North America and Australia, Connell argues that the issue of social justice is fundamental to what good education is about. If the school system deals unjustly with some of its pupils, the quality of education for all of the others is degraded. He calls for "curricular justice," which opens out the perspective of the least advantaged, roots itself in a democratic context, and moves toward the creation of a more equalitarian society. (Issue #28)

Here's What's Coming In Future Issues Of Our Schools/Our Selves

Articles On:

What Do We Tell Our Kids About Canada? — Environmental Activism — Unionizing ESL Teachers — The Failure Of The NDP To Initiate Education Reform In B.C., Saskatchewan And Ontario — The B.C. School Wars Continue — Labour, Education And The Arts — Sex In Upper Canada's Classrooms — Young Women In Trades — Education Politics In Alberta — Whatever Happened To York University? — A Letter From Siberia

You'll get three journals and three books a year for each subscription.

Books On:

Sex in Schools — Transition From School To Work — A Socialist-Feminist Approach To Phys. Ed. — Alternative Schools; Alternative Curriculum — Whatever Happened To High School History? — Australian Education Activism — What's Basic? A Democratic Socialist Strategy For Canada's Schools — Racism and Education — What Do People Really Think About Our Schools?

It's a great bargain, as much as 50% off the newstand price.

Subscribe Today

OUR SCHOOLS / OUR SELVES

Bringing together education activists in our schools, our communities and our unions...*with your help* !

Please enter my subscription for 6 issues of OUR SCHOOLS/OUR SELVES starting with issue number_____. Please check one:

INDIVIDUAL		ORGANIZATION	
____ Regular rate	$34.00	____ In Canada	$50.00
____ Student/Unemployed/		____ Outside Canada	Cdn $60.00
Pensioner rate	$28.00	**SUSTAINING**	
____ Outside Canada	Cdn $46.00	____ $100 ____ $200 Other $____	

OR send me issue number(s) _____ at $9.00 per single and $16.00 per double issue

Name_____

Address_____

City_____ Prov_____ Code_____

Occupation_____

___ Cheque enclosed ___ Bill me later ___ VISA / Mastercard

Card No_____ Expiry date _____

Signature_____

Pass to a friend

OUR SCHOOLS / OUR SELVES

Bringing together education activists in our schools, our communities and our unions...*with your help* !

Please enter my subscription for 6 issues of OUR SCHOOLS/OUR SELVES starting with issue number_____. Please check one:

INDIVIDUAL		ORGANIZATION	
____ Regular rate	$34.00	____ In Canada	$50.00
____ Student/Unemployed/		____ Outside Canada	Cdn $60.00
Pensioner rate	$28.00	**SUSTAINING**	
____ Outside Canada	Cdn $46.00	____ $100 ____ $200 Other $____	

OR send me issue number(s) _____ at $9.00 per single and $16.00 per double issue

Name_____

Address_____

City_____ Prov_____ Code_____

Occupation_____

___ Cheque enclosed ___ Bill me later ___ VISA / Mastercard

Card No_____ Expiry date _____

Signature_____

**Business
Reply Mail**

No postage stamp
necessary if mailed
in Canada.

Postage will be paid by

OUR SCHOOLS/OUR SELVES
1698 Gerrard Street East,
Toronto, Ontario, CANADA
M4L 9Z9

49261

**Business
Reply Mail**

No postage stamp
necessary if mailed
in Canada.

Postage will be paid by

OUR SCHOOLS/OUR SELVES
1698 Gerrard Street East,
Toronto, Ontario, CANADA
M4L 9Z9

49261